'Chizor's story is most compelling and inspiring. From war-ravaged Biafra to the leafy suburbs of Welwyn Garden City, from a child born with a disability to a woman who has found fulfilment as a leader in her community, a wife and a mother, Chizor's journey is one of refusing to accept limitations and believing that it is possible to overcome life's challenges. Her faith is her obvious strength. Refreshingly honest, bold and yet vulnerable, this book is commended to anyone who refuses to be held back.'

Agu Irukwu, Senior Pastor, Jesus House London

'In a light tone, with plenty of humour and wry observations, Chizor Akisanya tells the story of growing up with a disability in Nigeria and in England. We follow her from childhood, to adolescence to womanhood, to wifehood to motherhood, watching as she comes to terms with her endless potential and boundless possibilities along the way. Hers is the story of a victorious life, with diapers changed, cars driven, babies fed, exams passed, prayers answered, hurdles scaled (literally) and battles won every day. I dare you not to be inspired by this book.'

Chibundu Onuzo, author of **The Spider King's Daughter**

'This poetically written book reflects the grace and courage with which Chizor lives her life. This book will bring life, encouragement and challenge, not only to those who carry an obvious physical scar, but also to all those who struggle to feel like they belong.

'Chizor has learned to walk with confidence despite the challenges life has placed in her path. In these pages, she allows herself to be incredibly vulnerable and, in doing so, gives you a glimpse into how she has discovered the liberating truth that she is complete in Christ.'

Ian Hamilton, Chief Executive Officer, Compassion UK

'Once started, you will not put this book down. Chizor writes her story with candour, vulnerability and wisdom. From war-time injury and an education disrupted by operations, to inspirational teachers, work and a happy marriage and children, but also with the tragedy of the loss of two babies. This is an inspirational tale of a real life, lived with trust in the love and sovereignty of God.

'Her independence and determination never to be held back are striking, as is her frequent withdrawal into herself, into her own thoughts and talks with or at God. Chizor tells of the protection given by her parents, and especially her brothers, from a Nigerian culture which at that time rejected physically disabled people. She learns much in how to receive, from her marriage to Bajo and from the girls, from being part of a church family, right down to the kindness of those who braid her children's hair.

'Chizor is ever expectant of healing and does not doubt God's ability to do a miracle, but rejects the need and realises the harm done by chasing every speaker who promises a miracle healing. She lives each day for the blessings it brings.

'Chizor's injury was borne of the Biafra War. Looking at our world of conflicts, her story is timely and needs to be in the hands of today's children who are being physically and psychologically scarred by warfare.'

Baroness Elizabeth Berridge of the Vale of Catmose

'This is an uplifting meditation on Christianity and disability, by an author with a malfunctioning arm whose faith and determination have overcome many obstacles to a full life. Her advice to others, based on her own experience, will encourage them to put aside self-pity and achieve the very best they can.'

Richard Bourne, Senior Research Fellow, Institute of Commonwealth Studies, University of London; author of Nigeria: A New History of a Turbulent Century

'*Complete in Him* is a book of grace that not only opens up and tells a story; it also opens the reader's heart and mind to be inspired and changed. It is a story of hope in the face of adversity, told without self-pity or gloom, and Chizor's clarity, gentleness, strength and courage reveal the captivating adventure that happens when we are willing to say YES to God, despite our limitations. I warn you to read it with a box of tissues nearby and to be prepared for its wisdom to heal, challenge and inspire you. Readers will find *Complete in Him* to be an invitation to offer up your own hopes and weaknesses to God and see what extraordinary treasures He will bring about in you.'
Reverend Joanna Jepson, Anglican Priest, former Chaplain to the London College of Fashion and author of A Lot Like Eve: Fashion, Faith and Fig-Leaves: A Memoir

'This is a powerful story which is shared with vulnerability and poise, and one that leaves me deeply encouraged and inspired!

'This engaging narrative is a guide for us all to allow Christ to more fully dwell in our weaknesses, whatever we see them as in the face of the stranger around us. Chizor demonstrates powerfully how God has a plan and purpose no matter what challenges, events or supposed limitations we have.

'Here is a transforming encounter for those who live with physical and psychological challenges, prejudice and self-doubt. The triumph of this story is that overcoming challenges is possible, and Chizor demonstrates this through her bravery, meekness and endeavour of faith.'
The Reverend Terry Tennens, Chief Executive, International Justice Mission UK

'What an important message this book brings! Chizor Akisanya beautifully and bravely shares her story of the struggles disability presented to her and her resolute determination not to allow it to define her or hold her back from realising her full potential. It is a bold message of challenge to the wider community, including the church, that those with disabilities are to be embraced and not hidden. Rather they are to be cheered on at every stage of their journey to become fully who God created them to be, and recognising the tension between the pursuit of God's healing and wholeness on the one hand and the need to live life to the full "as we are" on the other.

'As someone who has known the considerable challenge of disability in my own life, I found Chizor's honesty both moving and inspirational. This book will be key in changing attitudes in the church – here is a new champion and voice to say that everyone has a contribution to make!'

Jennifer O'Brien, Solicitor and a Leader of King's Gate London

'Chizor Akisanya raises critical, thought-provoking life experiences that have long concerned all of us in all walks of life, with or without disabilities. How do you face everyday fears, big and small, and still walk on to succeed in any challenge, any day, anywhere? Chizor's touching, moving, poignant account of her life as a beautiful child and then beautiful woman with a disability makes such impressive sense as she reaches out to all of us with her stories. All readers, whether religious or not, will find much to stimulate their thoughts and provoke emotions buried deep within.'

Emma Edhem, CC, Deputy Head of International Law, Barrister No 5 Chambers; Common Councilman, City of London Corporation; Chairman Turkish British Chamber of Commerce and Industry

Complete in Him

Finding hope in disability and child loss

Chizor Akisanya

instant apostle

First published in Great Britain by Instant Apostle, 2016.

Instant Apostle

The Barn
1 Watford House Lane
Watford
Herts
WD17 1BJ

Every effort has been made to seek permission to use copyright material reproduced in this book. The publisher apologises for those cases where permission might not have been sought and, if notified, will formally seek permission at the earliest opportunity.

The views and opinions expressed in this work are those of the author and do not necessarily reflect the views and opinions of the publisher.

British Library Cataloguing-in-Publication Data

A catalogue record for this book is available from the British Library

This book and all other Instant Apostle books are available from Instant Apostle:

Website: www.instantapostle.com

E-mail: info@instantapostle.com

ISBN 978-1-909728-41-7

Printed in Great Britain

Complete in Him...

Now may the God of peace who brought up our Lord Jesus from the dead, that great Shepherd of the sheep, through the blood of the everlasting covenant, make you complete in every good work to do His will, working in you what is well pleasing in His sight, through Jesus Christ, to whom *be* glory forever and ever.

Amen.

Hebrews 13:20–21 (NKJV)

Contents

Dedication

This book is dedicated to the countless people, young and old, living with a disability; to those who feel that they are often overlooked in a world in which a message of physical perfection pervades many aspects of life. My hope is that as you read of my experiences, the process of renewing your mind will begin and you will in time come to an understanding of your true value in Christ. Jesus said: 'I have come that they may have life, and that they may have *it* more abundantly' (John 10:10, NKJV). Abundant life means a life of maximised potential, of complete fulfilment; when one employs one's gifts for the benefit of others. It is my prayer that you will redefine your boundaries, extending them by reaching for new heights and goals. I hope fervently that you will begin to dream again, dreams which are not constrained by circumstance, and that those dreams will gradually become reality. I thank the Lord for using me to reach His people and for showing me that I am *Complete in Him*.

Acknowledgements

With thanks…

To my husband, Bajo, who is my greatest cheerleader; I love you more than words can say. I am glad that we are on this great adventure together, and I look forward to a lifetime conquering new terrain with you by my side.

To my girls, Risachi (Sach) and Rinnah (Rinny). Thank you for your patience as I learned to care for you. Through the years, the sound of your voices calling me is a constant reminder of the faithfulness of our heavenly Father. You are growing into such beautiful young ladies, and I hope that your father and I have taught you to love the Lord as we love Him.

To my parents, Professor Joseph and Mrs Enoh Irukwu, you both encouraged me to dream, and to dream big. Daddy, you always made me feel very special and gave me my first picture of 'the Father's love'. Mummy, I remember all our trips to hospitals in search of a cure. Now that I have the girls, I appreciate even more the sacrifices you made. You were an incredible mother, and we all are blessed to have been shaped by such gentle hands.

To my siblings. My big brothers, Agu and Ikechi. Agu, our childhood battles helped develop my fighting spirit. You constantly remind me of that fighting spirit as I have gone through difficult situations as an adult, urging me to fight, and fight again. I love you and I am very proud of you.

Ikechi, you were always there when we were growing up. Our closeness in age meant that we shared many of life's experiences. You always looked out for me and never left my side when we were in public. I remember the jokes about us being the shirt and the sleeves! I am thankful for you.

And to my sisters, Chioma and Ola. Chioma, many years ago you saw my frustration and did endless research into driving schools for disabled drivers; you found my driving instructor and were elated when I passed my test at the first attempt. You have always encouraged me, always believed in me, sometimes even more than I believe in myself. My successes are your successes.

To Ola, my Spe, you let me practise parenting on you long before Risachi and Rinnah came along. And later you informed me that I was now your mother after Mummy passed on. I pray that your husband has an even bigger heart than Baj, and I look forward to giving you away... in a dress!

Words cannot express my gratitude to the Lord for the family that I have. I love you all and thank you from the bottom of my heart.

To Reverend Eastwood Anaba, thank you for writing the foreword to this book and for speaking into my life.

To those people whose names I don't know, those victors of the thalidomide nightmare who have overcome the adversity of their circumstances and are living purpose-filled lives. Your courage and determination teach me that I have no excuse!

To all the special people who have encouraged me to reach for the unreachable. Peter Broadhurst, my art teacher, who taught me never to give up. You showed me that there is always a way: you just have to be determined enough to find it. David Marshall, my English teacher, who saw my potential, and was determined that I would realise it. It was great to have an opportunity to meet up with you again almost three decades later and to show you what I have become.

Foreword

This book comes at a time when millions of people are struggling with diverse challenges all over the world. *Complete in Him* is the true story of Chizor Akisanya – a woman who has chosen to celebrate her scars. She has not disguised her physical challenge, neither has she denied its existence. Instead she has overcome the limitations imposed on her through the brachial plexus injury to her right arm.

We all have scars in one form or the other. These scars must not make us feel inferior. Our scars can generate momentum in us instead of inertia, if our attitude is right.

Here is what Golda Meir, one of the founders of the state of Israel and its fourth Prime Minister, had to say about her lack of great beauty – her scars: 'Not being beautiful was the true blessing. Not being beautiful forced me to develop my inner resources. The pretty girl has a handicap to overcome.' (Golda Meir, 1898–1978[1]) She refused to be limited by how others looked at her.

Chizor has been honest enough to share the pain of being physically challenged. She talks about trying to hide her limb – putting her arm behind her or in her pocket to cover it up as often as she can. Nevertheless, she is living a very fulfilled life. When I first met her, it took me a while to notice her challenge. Her confidence, radiance and brilliance overpowered her scars.

Three things make Chizor unique:

- She believes that God will heal her. Never stop believing God to turn things around for you.

- She has developed her potential in ministry, career and family. She is still pursuing excellence.

- The joy of the Lord is visible in every aspect of her life as she seeks to encourage others.

We celebrate Chizor for using her life to speak into millions of lives – this book is medicine to millions. I see it releasing the champion in you as you read it.

Eastwood Anaba
Founder of Eastwood Anaba Ministries

---

[1] Golda Meir, cited in Jerry Parr, Carolyn Parr, *In the Secret Service: The True Story of the Man Who Saved Ronald Reagan* (Tyndale House Publishers, 2013), chapter 7.

Introduction

I first started writing this book sometime in 2003. At the time I felt I had a story that might help someone going through a similar experience. The first draft was completed in 2004, but then for some reason it got shelved. I began having second thoughts about whether I wanted to expose myself to this extent. I doubted whether anyone would be interested in reading about my life, and succeeded in talking myself out of going forward and having it published.

In the years following I focused on other areas of my life and career and went on to do a range of things, but I never stopped writing, and people who knew of the existence of this draft kept asking me when I would publish the book. Over the years I have written other books, all as yet unpublished. I knew I had to take the final step towards conclusion, and I was faced with the question of which book to complete first. Unsurprisingly, I focused on the book that seemed closest to the end, which was not this book. But then I had the most interesting experience.

One day an American evangelist, a wonderful lady called Prophetess Francina Norman, spoke to a group of which I was a part. As she was wrapping up, and without warning, she turned to me and said, 'I just hear the Lord say that you've got to write this book. He says you've been procrastinating ... but you have to write this book ... And it needs to be finished this year.' I was so startled because this lady had no idea of the circumstances of my life or the issues that I grappled with at the time. Although there were other books, her statement left me in no doubt as to the particular book to which she referred. My husband's words a few days later were the confirmation that I needed. I had just narrated to him details of the incident with the visiting minister: 'That's settled, then,' he said. '*Complete in Him*, it is.'

He went on to remind me of what he had said a decade earlier. At that time he had read the first draft and his initial comment was that I seemed to be holding back. He thought that I needed to be more open, that my writing was guarded and restrained. I knew exactly what he meant, but I was not able to let down my defences to the extent that he indicated. With time, I have matured in my relationship with Jesus; I have grown and come to a place of greater self-acceptance and inner peace. I realise even more than I did previously that this is something that is clearly bigger than I am; I must overcome whatever insecurities I have about its contents and write openly and honestly.

Prophetess Norman said that it would bring healing to many people, myself included, and so I submit myself to be used by the Lord exactly as He wills. I am grateful for a loving Father who does not write us off but waits patiently for us to catch up with Him. I am deeply humbled that He would use me at all, that He would wait a decade for me to get my act together, and I pray that this book does bring healing to those who need it.

Chizor Akisanya

Preface

Write all the words that I have spoken to you in a book.
(Jeremiah 30:2)

Before I set out to write this book, I was reminded of these words that the Lord had spoken to me some time earlier. The meaning could not have been any clearer: 'Write all the words that I have spoken to you in a book.' At another time, I opened up the Bible one morning, not really looking for anything; my fingers simply opened up the book. I glanced at the pages and a verse appeared, like I was looking at it through a magnifying glass. The words were big and bold and appeared to jump off the page: 'Write the things which you have seen, and the things which are, and the things which will take place after this' (Revelation 1:19, NKJV).

Throughout my life, I have kept a journal, although not always diligently, and there are periods when entries are somewhat sporadic. At difficult periods I have found writing to be cathartic, an outlet for pent-up feelings and emotions and a way of attaining peace. I have always had a strong urge to record events, successes and failures. Writing has been another means by which I communicate with the Lord and through which I have received strength. My journals have become my private reservoir of memories that continue to feed my faith.

At a very early age, when I first became aware of the potential limitations of a disability, I made a practical decision. I remember thinking that I could not change my situation, therefore it was pointless dwelling on it and getting depressed. I then decided to get on with living life to the best of my ability. I was unprepared for the impact of a disability on my ability to 'live life fully', but I was also unacquainted with the life-changing experience of knowing Jesus Christ as my Lord and Saviour. As I have got to know Him better, I realise that although I am physically limited, paradoxically, there are no limitations on my ability to reach my potential.

I have written this book through the leading of the Lord for that special person living with a physical disability or disfigurement, anything that marks the individual and affects their or other people's perception of them. It is also relevant for anyone living with other less visible disabilities – anything that prevents a person from being their real self, attacking their confidence and sense of worth. As you read of my experiences in living with a disability, I hope that you will be challenged to dare to dream and to reach for greater heights, just as I have. The following excerpt from a book I once read sums up my motivation for writing this book. It brought home to me the reason I feel so strongly about attempting to present an alternative path to someone living with a 'disability' (and I use this term cautiously).

The Bible tells of how God used a prophet, a man called Ezekiel, to bring a message of hope to a demoralised group of people who were exiled from their homeland. But before he did, God wanted him to experience first hand the people's pain and dejection.

In reference to this commissioning of Ezekiel, bestselling author and preacher John Hagee writes:

God wanted to communicate with these refugees, these Jewish people who had been kicked out of their homes. So He sent Ezekiel down there to sit with them for seven days until he knew how they felt. Only then was Ezekiel commissioned to speak the words of God. Ezekiel said, 'I sat where they sat' (Ezekiel 3.15).

Don't tell me you know how I feel if you've never experienced what I am experiencing. Ezekiel went out and became a captive. He went to live in exile with the refugees. He let the blows of humiliation fall on his back. He looked at the world through their eyes, with all of his possessions on his back, without security and without hope. 'I sat where they sat'. I got the feeling of what they really feel.[1]

One sentence struck a chord in my heart: 'Don't tell me you know how I feel if you've never experienced what I am experiencing.' For those who may identify with these feelings of insecurity and hopelessness, I have sat where you now sit, I have felt and still feel what you feel, and I can say that Jesus will make a difference if only you allow Him.

---

[1] John Hagee, *Communication in Marriage* (San Antonio, Global Evangelism Publishing, 1991) p.26.

Chapter one
The beginning

God said, Let Us, [Father, Son and Holy Spirit] make mankind
in Our image, after Our likeness, and let them have complete
authority ... And God saw everything that He had made, and
behold, it was very good (suitable, pleasant) *and* He approved
it completely.
(Genesis 1:26, 31)

Value is dictated and indicated by source. Value may also be
dictated by uniqueness and rarity. The more unique a substance,
the more valuable it is, and consequently, the more sought-after
it is. Our source is the Lord. There is no creation more valuable
than humankind, none as unique as we are; we each are originals,
created by God for a specific purpose. Each person is special.
You are neither insignificant nor worthless. Regardless of our
flaws or failings, God loves each of us exactly as we are, *but* I
have come to realise that He loves us too much to leave us the
way we are.[1]

'God saw everything that He had made, and behold, it was
very good ... *and* He approved it completely.' I preface this first
chapter with this bold statement of truth because it is the
foundation upon which this book rests.

I was born in the eastern part of Nigeria during tumultuous times, at the start of the Nigerian civil war.[2] It was a time of horror and uncertainty, when the weak and vulnerable suffered greatly. My parents and two older brothers, along with countless others, having been displaced, returned to the eastern part of Nigeria as refugees in their own country. Mum and Dad originated from eastern Nigeria, but like many young professionals they had made their home in what was the capital city, Lagos, which is on the western coast. Nigeria in those days was in her fledgling years. The euphoria of independence had fizzled out like air from a day-old helium balloon, leaving behind a sad reality, which was several failed attempts at peaceful coexistence by a group of very diverse people whose differences were far more than anything they had in common. As time went on, these differences became even more glaring and an already severely strained fabric began to disintegrate irreparably. The final spiral towards war came through a series of events of civil disorder and mayhem, including the mass killing of eastern Nigerians living and working in northern Nigeria.

For a time, Lagos as the federal capital remained relatively safe for the easterners who had made their home there, but the situation soon turned, and as the months passed it became increasingly dangerous to live there. In time there began a country-wide exodus of easterners from all walks of life returning to their states of origin, and before long the eastern region, under the leadership of a charismatic young soldier,[3] declared its independence from Nigeria. The state of Biafra was born and war was official. In the days and weeks following, my parents and other refugees attempted to survive amidst dropping bombs, hunger, and disease, one of which was *kwashiorkor*,[4] caused by protein deficiency. Little was known about this disease prior to the Nigerian Civil War. It was not the best time for a child to be born.

The day of my birth, the war raging from without appeared to be mirrored within as my mother struggled with an extended and complicated labour which had lasted two days. An area close to the hospital in which I was born came under attack. Bombs rained down, scattering chaos and confusion as she went into labour. It was a frightening and bewildering time. There is something disturbingly surreal about a very normal event, such as giving birth, occurring in the midst of death and devastation.

Things took an even worse turn for my mother, and an emergency Caesarean section, for which the medical staff were unprepared, resulted in me sustaining a brachial plexus injury (to my right arm), which occurs when the nerves controlling muscles in the arm and shoulder are damaged.[5] With so much destruction around, our survival against the odds was truly remarkable. My parents named me Chizor (which in the Ibo language, spoken largely by south-easterners, means 'God saves') in acknowledgement of the miraculous nature of my arrival.

In time they took me home. The future was uncertain, but we were alive and we were all together. Life took on our new normal – my mother returned to her position at the broadcasting house of the new country, and my father continued as legal adviser to the Red Cross. In the continual upheaval of constantly being on the run, moving from one city to the next as the opposing forces (the federal troops) advanced, desperately trying to stay alive, and with a rapidly crumbling medical infrastructure, the injury I had sustained at birth remained undetected. But as the days and weeks went by, my mother noticed that there was something unusual about the way my arm hung and my obvious preference for one arm over the other. I was only a few months old at the time. In the chaotic environment there was little that could be done and no one to whom she could turn with her fears. Understandably, the focus at the time was on keeping our young family together and more importantly, on staying alive.

Almost three years later, the war was over. We had lost most of our property, but remarkably we were all well, although like countless families we had not been untouched by the experience. Mum and Dad talked about the challenge of living in such uncertainty; you could see someone one day and the next day they might be dead. With so many babies and children dying from bombs, flying shrapnel, famine and sickness, it was a miracle that we had survived when more than a million civilians were dead.

Upon the cessation of military conflict, Biafra ceased to exist and the eastern region was reabsorbed into the fold, becoming part of Nigeria once again. Mum and Dad were faced with the uphill task of rebuilding our lives from scratch. We returned to Lagos from where the family had fled three years earlier. Some dear friends of my parents, John and Monica Hutton, a wonderful Caribbean couple, put us up in their home for several months. It was a huge sacrifice to provide a haven for a shell-shocked family of five with very young children who were still plagued by the sounds of war. Whenever a plane flew past, my brothers would dive underneath the nearest bed and bury their heads in their arms.

'Under the bed!' they would scream, echoing the instructions that had been a regular part of our lives for so many months.

It took a long time for the grown-ups to convince them that it was safe to come out, and even longer for them to stop being fearful of the drone of passing planes. My father was able to return to his work as legal adviser for an insurance company, and my mother returned to the Broadcasting Corporation as

Director of Programmes. Soon they moved us into our own home and began the process of carving out a normal existence.

For the first time since my birth, they were able to seek formal medical opinion concerning me. I was three years old. It was then that they were given a proper diagnosis, then that they learned the sad fact that the injury that occurred could have been easily treatable but for the war and the prevailing circumstances. They also learned that whilst we had highly skilled doctors who had been trained at some of the best institutions around the world, the hospitals were poorly equipped and unable to perform the reconstructive surgeries that were required. This was the beginning of my interaction with medical personnel and hospitals that lasted decades.

In one twist of fate, as a result of a series of events which no one could have predicted, damage had occurred. As a direct consequence, I have very limited mobility and control in my right arm, which is considerably smaller than the other.

This is my story.

My story

My early childhood was characterised by a lack of awareness that I was in any way different from other children; I was happy, confident and completely at ease with myself. My arrival after two boys had been greeted with great joy and excitement. I held the cherished position of '*Ada*', or first daughter, which is a position of great privilege amongst my people, the Ibos. I was very close to my parents and share a particularly strong bond with my father. He doted on me and was unapologetic in his devotion. Similarly, my mum was sacrificial in her care of all her children. She was the proverbial lioness who would react vigorously to any attack on her cubs! We were loved and we all, without exception, knew it well. Unknown to us then, the combination of our parents' love would give us a strength of character that we would not fully appreciate until we became adults.

I could not have asked for a better family. I was like a creature in a cocoon and well aware of the protective shield surrounding me, even when I was very small. One of the very early duties my father had assigned to my brothers was the responsibility of 'taking care' of the household whenever he was away from home, which was often. When he would call home he would ask each of them in turn, 'How is your mother? How is your sister? Are you taking care of everything?' They took their responsibility very seriously, even though they were only five and seven years old respectively. What followed would be a detailed or vague report, depending on which brother was the reporter.

For my part, I flourished in the midst of the attention. I followed my brothers around like the proverbial shadow, ratted on them when it suited me, was the quintessential pest, but also a most determined student. They were my world. I learned everything very early and very eagerly and notched up childhood conquests with great rapidity. I could climb trees faster than many boys my age and definitely any girl in the neighbourhood. I learned to ride a bicycle that was meant for someone twice my age when I was only four. I remember that I could not reach the pedals if I sat on the seat, and so I learned to ride standing, and even graduated to waving my arm around whilst shouting, 'Look! No hands!' My control was very dodgy in the beginning and there were many mishaps. Each time I collided with a neighbour's bin or a tree that 'just wouldn't get out of my way', it was as though I was receiving my badge of honour when I was extricated from twisted metal with bleeding knees and elbows and not a tear in sight!

The word 'tomboy' was bandied around often. I dressed accordingly in shorts and T-shirts and scoffed at anything girly. I was a willing addition to any football team, even if I was only allowed to play on the rare occasions that they were short of players. And though the only available position was goalkeeper, because no one else wanted it, my enthusiasm was not dampened. I was desperate to be included, and it was a great privilege for a five-year-old girl to play with the big boys. During the games, I threw my little body left and right, bending and twisting like a trapeze artist; nothing was as important as ensuring that that piece of leather did not sneak past me. Whenever I made a save, I was hoisted up on to someone's bony shoulders and my arm was grasped and thrust upwards in a victorious pump. My joy was complete.

One Christmas, one of my brothers got two sets of boxing gloves as a gift, and a corner of our back garden became a boxing ring. Before long I learned to box, discovering that I had what my brother Agu, who was my trainer, described as a super left hook, followed by a knockout upper cut. Very soon, he was organising 'exhibition matches', and I was the star act! Although I never had any proof of this, I suspect that he would charge the neighbourhood kids a fee, but I never saw the proceeds of my labour. Today he has conveniently forgotten.

Those years were exciting and uncomplicated, the stuff that children's adventure stories are made of. All the while, I was loved and fiercely protected. I never felt that I was different, and any child daring to suggest that there was anything different about me was in danger of becoming acquainted with big brother's ready fists. In fact, I recall Agu's swift reaction when one child called me a derogatory name. That was the only time that I remember being picked on. I have no recollection of ever feeling self-conscious or inadequate when I was very young. I was just like any other child, relating to others on a level playing field. But then I grew up and life became less simple. I began to question my difference; why did I have this arm that did not work? Why had it happened to me?

Increasingly, as I moved from childhood to adolescence and early adulthood, every day became a challenge – a challenge to understand and appreciate the true meaning of my life; a challenge to remain unmarked by bitterness and anger; a challenge to appreciate my true value. To this day, I still encounter challenges, albeit of a slightly different kind. I liken my life to a journey on the long road of discovery – I am yet to arrive at my destination, but an encounter with Jesus along the way has steered me in the right direction, has made available, and continues to make available, the strength for the journey, and most importantly has guaranteed a successful outcome. With each passing day I am coming progressively to a realisation of my true worth.

I do not in any way profess to have all the answers, but this one thing I know: Jesus has made a tremendous difference to my life. Whilst I have some understanding, I cannot claim to fully understand why I have this disability. Interestingly, the reason is now irrelevant – I am increasingly developing a sense of personal worth. I know I have an important contribution to make, and by striving to be the best that I can be in my circumstances, I will be a faithful steward of the life that has been granted to me.

---

[1] A sentiment expressed by John Mason: 'God loves you just the way you are, but He loves you too much to leave you the way you are.' From *You're Born An Original; Don't Die a Copy* (Oklahoma, Insight International, 1993).

---

[2] Nigeria is a federation of 36 states and a Federal Capital Territory with approximately 500 ethnic groups of which the Yoruba, Ibo and Hausa/Fulani are the three major groups. The west is dominated by the Yorubas, the east by the Ibos and the north by the Hausa/Fulani. The country's boundaries had been defined arbitrarily by the colonial powers that had formerly controlled the region. Nigeria became independent of British rule in October 1960, but escalating tensions between the ethnic groups culminated in the attempted secession of the south-eastern provinces of Nigeria as the Republic of Biafra only six and a half years later on 30th May 1967. The war that resulted lasted for two and a half years between mid-1967 and early 1970. There were 100,000 military casualties and an estimated one million civilian deaths from starvation.

[3] Lt Col Chukwuemeka Odumegwu Ojukwu, leader of the Republic of Biafra from 30th May 1967 to 15th January 1970.

[4] Kwashiorkor was a rare form of protein deficiency which became very common in Biafra. It was a wasting disease that attacked the muscles and caused a swelling of the belly. In addition to the characteristic distended abdomen, sufferers, who were mainly children, had stick-like legs and arms and hair that turned a reddish, terracotta colour. By early 1968, less than nine months after the war started, there were approximately 300,000 child sufferers of the disease, according to a fact-finding mission of the International Committee of the Red Cross.

[5] A brachial plexus injury (Erb's Palsy) occurs when the nerves that control muscles in the shoulder, arm or hand are damaged; these nerves may sometimes be paralysed. Most brachial plexus injuries occur during birth, with an estimated one in two newborn babies out of 1,000 sustaining such injuries.

Chapter two
You are beautiful

For You did form my inward parts; You did knit me together in
my mother's womb ... My frame was not hidden from You
when I was being formed in secret ... Your eyes saw my
unformed substance, and in Your book all the days [of my life]
were written before ever they took shape ...
(Psalm 139:13–16)

In stark contrast to my carefree childhood, my adolescent years
were difficult. That period was as night following day. I am not
sure how the change happened, but somewhere around starting
secondary school things began to turn. I attended a girls-only
Catholic day school in a leafy suburb in Lagos which I loved
from the very beginning. I had just turned ten years old when I
joined the school. On my first day I met Linda, a mischievous
girl with skin the colour of creamy tea, a mop of untamed brown
curls and a tongue as sharp as a new razor. We hit it off
immediately, and she became my friend for life. We were
opposites in many respects. She was very popular, outspoken
and unrestrained, full of the mischief of youth and bent on
driving as many nuns as possible to near distraction. She was
great fun! She seemed to spend an inordinate amount of time in
detention outside the principal's office for a raft of infractions

for which she was totally unrepentant. One exasperated teacher, learning of our friendship, once warned that she would 'lead me astray'. I, of course, failed to heed her warning. Like so many people whose paths have crossed mine, she was a clear Godsend. Many times throughout our secondary school years she drew me out of myself, and would never take no for an answer. As we navigated the meandering and often confusing path of adolescence, she was my steady companion.

We had a boys' Catholic secondary school a street across from ours, and at the end of each school day the boys and girls would hang out together for as long as they could keep their waiting drivers from hauling them off home. My friend would always stay close by. She was feisty and carefree and determined to pull me along, despite my resistance. She always had a bevy of pubescent admirers hanging on her every word, and I was struck by her confidence and ease. I remember that she was the bearer of my very first 'love note'; a crumpled letter complete with ink splodges and handwriting that resembled hieroglyphics, courtesy of an awkward 11-year-old boy from our 'brother-school' who penned a most unoriginal poem that went something like this: *'Roses are red, violets are blue, sugar is sweet and so are you! Will you be my Valentine?'* Whilst I was unimpressed by his lack of literary prowess, his request was a great boost to the confidence of a painfully shy pre-teen. It was also the only one that I got, and I kept it for a very long time.

We also had something called the Literary and Debating Society at junior and senior levels (abbreviated to Junior Lits and Senior Lits). Alongside the debating which, as far as the students were concerned, was a good excuse for socialising, there were opportunities to meet up and form romantic connections. The different schools in the city took it in turns to host the debating societies, and busloads of students would be ferried across school campuses. For weeks on end in the run-up to these events, there would be non-stop discussions on who was coming from the various schools and who was dating whom. The focus was always on the dance that took place after the formalities of debating were over. We were restricted to wearing school uniform, but the girls found innovative ways of stretching the boundaries in order to make themselves stand out. Hemlines were redefined and regulation skirts lost several inches overnight. Blouses appeared to have shrunk and become like a second skin, and because this was inappropriate appearance for good convent schoolgirls there was, preceding these events, a cat-and-mouse game as the girls tried to escape the scrutiny of the more eagle-eyed staff who were on the lookout for serial skirt-hitchers. Getting caught would open up the real possibility of being barred from attending, but the aim was to be memorable, and it was worth the risk!

I tried as much as possible to avoid these events and for this reason shied away from the debating team, but the few times that I did go, I remember, were like tests of my endurance. Whilst I loved music and did not mind clowning around with my sisters in the safe confines of our home, I was no dancer, certainly not of the calibre of my friends, whose bodies glided and popped and jerked in perfect harmony with whatever sound was blaring from oversized speakers. I struggled to keep up with the constant changes in dance moves that were exported from North America with memorable names like Electric Boogaloo, Running Man, Moonwalk, Cabbage Patch, and the Slide and Rock. The girls mastered every new move and were always geared up to demonstrate the latest additions to their repertoire. The highest accolade was to be recognised as someone who was 'current' as opposed to 'stale'. My entire stock, on the other hand, consisted of a two-step side shuffle, at two speeds – fast and slow – depending on what was playing. Needless to say this was an unmistakable clue to my paucity in that area. But the dances were the obligatory rite of passage, and so I went in silent protest.

The boys lined up alongside one wall of the vast assembly hall with the girls similarly arranged on the opposite side. Boys trying to look 'cool', elbowed one another, eyeing up the girls and then laying claim to the object of their attention. Having had their confidence stoked by the collective brotherhood, one by one they sidled across to the girls, stood in front of the one that piqued their interest and said in the deepest, 'coolest' voice they could muster, 'Would you like to dance?' Showing a distinct lack of interest, for it was an unspoken rule never to appear eager, the particular girl would look the boy up and down as though sizing him up, and then respond with a casual 'sure' or 'no thank you', depending on whether he ticked enough of the right boxes. Then the boy would either lead her in triumph to the middle of the dance floor, or embark on the lonely walk of shame, slinking back to his brothers to restrategise.

As the couples paired up, the bodies clinging to the wall reduced. Rejection is a horrible thing, particularly for a teenager. People lived in fear of being left hanging. But the truth was that the more popular, older-looking, generously endowed girls were picked first. With a frame that was more right-angled than curvy and a face that looked much younger than my 13 years, I did not believe that anyone would find me the least bit striking, and I loathed those long moments waiting to be picked, watching the numbers dwindle and trying to feign ease as I tapped my foot and mouthed lyrics. Although I was always picked eventually, it was seldom by any of the popular boys, and I figured that my partners were just as awkward and inept in the esoteric art of teenage socialising. They certainly did not inspire confidence. As a result, I withdrew into myself like a snail into its shell.

Looking back with the clarity of adulthood, I have a better understanding of the child and teen that I was, but at the time it was like walking around with a cloud hanging over me. What was worse was that I did not have the words to explain what was going on in my head even if anyone had asked me. I always had a sense that the real me was trapped somewhere. It often seemed as though there were two of me; one was a semi-recluse type who only found expression in my writing and in the music that I listened to. The other, which was the public face, seemed to function quite well on the outside, but in reality was like a complicated knot which just got more twisted as time went by. My happiness was interspersed with bouts of misery. Besides Linda, my curly-headed steady companion, I had several close friends at school, and my brothers were extremely popular, so our home was a hive of activity. But none of this shielded me from the darkness that seemed to be lurking around the corner. Without warning it would engulf me, almost like I had walked into a swirling mist. It would be triggered by anything from a careless comment delivered without tact to a situation that highlighted my difference.

'I have great plans for you'

During those dark days, I would spend hours in my bedroom listening to the most awful music which was generations older than I was; slow, haunting sounds that spoke of heartbreak, pain and despair. There was nothing uplifting about it, and I fed my mind with a steady diet of that junk. I would remain there, only interacting with my family when I was summoned to the dining table at mealtimes, a brooding, sullen teenager who responded

39

to questions in monosyllables. My parents had very busy schedules; they worked long hours, travelled a lot and were often away for days and sometimes weeks on end. We were tended by a slew of staff who made the household tick over like clockwork but lacked the skills or the awareness to draw out a struggling young girl whose situation was compounded by the complexities of adolescence and puberty. I did not think that I was attractive; I certainly did not feel attractive and was very uncomfortable in my skin. The knowledge that I was very special to my parents and that I was loved and cherished gave me confidence in certain areas, but at that time it was not enough. It did not erase those feelings of deep insecurity with which I battled.

Sometime later I had an experience that brought me great comfort. It became an experience that I would reach back to many times in the future. One day, I was having one of many conversations with Jesus. I had always had a strong sense of Him being there for as long as I could remember. It may have had something to do with my Christian upbringing or the fact that I went to a Catholic school, but almost unconsciously I found that I would always reach for where I could derive comfort at difficult times. I knew all the Bible stories that spoke of Jesus' love for little children; I had heard them all my life. I also remembered the songs that accompanied most of those stories.

There was a chapel at my secondary school and the nuns would hold Mass twice a day at 6.30 a.m. and 6.30 p.m. The morning Mass was held long before the school day began and the girls were not required to attend, although a few whose families were practising Catholics did. I found out about it quite by accident when I got to school extremely early one morning, and went in search of the reason for the chanting that floated across the courtyard in the crisp morning air. As I sat in a pew towards the rear of the chapel I felt a sense of peace descend on me like a warm blanket on a cold day. It was over much too soon, and I knew that I would return.

My challenge was that my brother Ikechi who attended the school across from mine was not keen on leaving home so early. He needed to be 'persuaded', and for a time I made it worth his while. Then I found out that some schoolfriends who lived in our neighbourhood left home pre-dawn because with five children attending three schools, there were several stops on the school run, and they began their day early so as to beat the traffic. I convinced my mother to let me go with them two days a week, and I began arriving at school early enough to attend Mass with the nuns.

Even though we were Anglicans, there was just something that drew me; I was comfortable saying the Hail Marys and comfortable dabbing my forehead with holy water as I went through the chapel, but my focus was always on the Lord Jesus. There was just something easy and effortless about our relationship. With Him I did not need to pretend; He could handle whatever dark thought that I had and He was not fazed by my meltdowns. When I was unable to communicate my thoughts to anyone, I felt that Jesus understood every unspoken word.

My conversation with Him that particular day had been triggered by an incident at a store checkout counter. My mum had sent me to pick up a few things at the store. Whilst the driver waited in the car park, I had nipped in to make the purchase. The lady at the checkout had just rung through my items, and I handed her the money. She looked at me and then looked pointedly at my hand holding the *naira* notes, saying nothing. Not thinking anything of it, I said, 'Here you are!', thrusting my hand forward. Her reaction threw me off-kilter.

'Why are you giving me something with your left hand? Use your right hand!' she hissed.

I froze.

I continued holding out my hand with the money in it. She glared at me, muttering under her breath about children who had no respect. Angry tears welled up in my eyes. I knew she was only behaving in this manner because I did not have an adult with me. A queue was forming behind me and in typical African fashion, people got involved; some took my side, telling the woman to take the money and leave me alone, but there was one voice that supported her behaviour. And that voice seemed to be louder than the rest. I wanted to say many disparaging things to her, but that would have been completely alien to me. We had been taught never to be rude to our elders; that is the African way... older people were always right, and a child never challenged an adult's authority. But I did glare at her in defiance, allowing myself that one pleasure. I hoped my eyes said the things that my lips could not. Without a word I walked out, leaving behind my shopping. Her angry voice and several eyes trailed me out of the store.

'Where are the things your mummy asked you to get? Didn't you see them?' asked the puzzled driver.

'Please take me home,' was my only reply.

Mum was out when we got to the house, and I went up to my room, slamming the door shut. Only then did I let out my pain and frustration.

I cried and cried.

'Why did You make me this way? WHY?'

Silence.

'Why haven't You healed me? I know You can, so why won't You?'

Silence.

'Did You hear what that nasty woman said to me?'

More silence.

'It's not fair!' I cried until my eyes stung and my pillow was soaked.

Then when I was completely spent, what seemed like a thought entered my mind.

'You are special. I have great plans for you.'

I will cherish these words forever.

I never told anyone about my experience at the shop. It was just another in a series of events that I had to learn to deal with. In that culture, it was regarded as a sign of rudeness to use your left hand; the left hand was thought to be forbidden, useful only for less 'noble' tasks. I reasoned that it was nothing personal, really; the woman did not know any better. Her behaviour was informed by her level of exposure. In fact, the cultural values were often discriminatory towards left-handed people. Culture was so ingrained that in some settings naturally left-handed children were forced to learn to write with their right hands. I have heard stories of children who were rapped across the knuckles for using their left hands, and one particularly horrible story of a child whose left hand was tied to his side so that he was compelled to use his right hand.

That was not a pleasant experience for me, but I recognise that some good came out of it. I now think nothing of fighting for anyone who is being treated badly, particularly if it happens to be a child.

About a year ago, I was at an open-day event where exhibitors showcase their services to members of the public. As I went from stand to stand, a lady that I slightly knew directed me to her stand. She had the most beautiful fabrics. I stood admiring her African prints; she said she wanted to introduce me to her partner. As though on cue, a second lady walked up to us. I turned to greet her, listening carefully as my acquaintance made the introductions. The lady stretched out her hand and I stretched out mine.

'No, no,' she said, shaking her head and admonishing me like a child. 'I insist that you use your right hand or I will not shake your hand.'

You could have knocked me over with a feather. This was not Africa, we were in London, and as far as I could tell this lady was not African! Next to me, I felt my acquaintance stiffen before I saw the look of absolute horror on her face. For a split second I was taken back to that childhood experience in the grocery store and those old, negative feelings threatened to resurface, but I was no longer a child; I am an adult, and I can stand up for myself! My recovery was swift. I smiled sweetly. 'Then I suppose we shall have to do away with the handshake!'

With that I swept past her, commended their merchandise and then moved on to the next stall. I could imagine the conversation that must have taken place in my wake. Much later on, my acquaintance apologised for her partner's presumptiveness; apparently she was a little outspoken. In the past, such a careless comment would have sent me into an emotional tailspin. But what I found interesting was the fact that I was not hurt or offended by her behaviour. In fact, it was something of a life lesson for me. From that experience I learned to be careful about making judgements; I learned that there is very often more to every situation than is initially apparent, and to observe first before making any comments. That day, I knew that I had definitely come a long way and that I had grown considerably.

Our experiences are for the benefit of someone else

I often wonder why I embarked on this project, considering the fact that I have always cherished my privacy. Many times, I have questioned my willingness to 'show my wounds', to openly discuss my pain and to reveal my vulnerability. But my conclusion is always that this is something God would have me do at this time in my life. And this realisation far exceeds any momentary discomfort that I may feel. Philippians 2:4 says: 'Don't look out only for your own interests, but take an interest in others, too.' (NLT) I have made a conscious decision to be a witness of the Lord's goodness and strength, regardless of my weaknesses or any other considerations. I have developed a strong desire to reach out to people experiencing similar challenges, and I truly believe that I am how I am for the benefit of someone else.

Our actions usually affect someone else – either positively or negatively. What we do, or fail to do, will always be a benefit or disadvantage to somebody else. Once I understood this, my thinking was transformed dramatically. I am now aware of the selfishness and futility of self-pity. I think of self-pity as little more than wasteful indulgence. Elisabeth Elliot, Christian author and missionary, who spent years as a missionary to an eastern Ecuadorean tribe that killed her first husband and lost her second husband to illness, wrote this about her losses: 'I know of nothing more paralyzing, more deadly, than self-pity. It is a death that has no resurrection, a sink-hole from which no rescuing hand can drag you because you have chosen to sink. But it must be refused. In order to refuse it, of course, I must recognize it for what it is.'[1]

45

I have learned to look outside my own circumstances to those of others, to take my eyes off me and focus on the ways that I could make a difference to someone else's life. My success at overcoming difficulties has an impact, albeit sometimes an indirect one, on another person's ability to overcome similar challenges. Many times our misery or pain becomes the very thing that provides a bridge to reach other people. I have found that we are better equipped to relate to someone who is experiencing pain that we have experienced; there is a sense of sharing, a common bond that allows access into a person's world. It requires a certain level of openness, a willingness to expose oneself. But being vulnerable is never easy; our inclination very often is to protect ourselves. We are usually careful to conceal our wounds and scars from the world, hiding behind masks of perfection which give no clues as to the chaos and turmoil that may lie within. However, one's scars are the marks that announce to the world that you are a survivor. Scars speak for you; they tell everyone in a split second your history, the fact that you have fought some battles and survived. And most importantly, they convey a silent message of hope to people who may have lost all hope. I am learning to embrace my scars without dwelling on them.

---

[1] Elisabeth Elliot, *Facing the Death of Someone You Love* (Crossway Books, 1980)

Chapter three
Growing pains: adolescent years

I discovered early that the hardest thing to overcome is not a
physical disability but the mental condition which it induces.
The world, I found, has a way of taking a man pretty much at
his own rating. If he permits his loss to make him
embarrassed and apologetic, he will draw embarrassment
from others. But if he gains his own respect, the respect of
those around him comes easily.
(Alexander de Seversky, Russian-American pilot and inventor,
1894–1974[1])

Every child's worst nightmare is to be different from their peers.
By adolescence, the desire for 'sameness' is almost an obsession.
Adolescents want to fit in with the crowd, to do nothing that will
cause them to be labelled as 'strange' or 'weird', and I was no
different. I had no desire to be different from other teenagers,
and I wanted to be able to do the same things they did. I never
wanted to be set apart, and I definitely never wanted to be the
focus of people's interests. But I was, and it made me very self-
conscious and uncomfortable. On the outside, I seemed to be
coping very well, and life continued to roll on. On the inside, I
was often unsure of myself, comfortable only in familiar
surroundings with people who knew me well.

I came from the kind of family where people exhibited
strength of character. We faced challenges with calm dignity; we
were not given to emotional outbursts; we thought rationally and
we spoke rationally, having weighed up all of our options. I

remember that my father taught us to process our 'strong argument', to reason things through and then present our case. On the rare occasions when anyone had an emotional 'episode', they would be viewed as though they had somehow lost their mind. Slammed doors and shouting fits never received the attention that they may perhaps have got in a different family setting. There was a very practical approach to love. Each child knew they were loved, but we were not told every minute that we were loved. We just knew it. There were very clear demonstrations of that love; we lacked nothing material. Everything we needed and more was provided generously. The ties that bound us were extremely strong; we talked about many things, and when we got together as a family, there was lots of laughter, lots of witty exchanges and many demonstrations of the strength of our unity. But we did not have conversations around emotions and feelings. Those appeared to be no-go areas. And yet we were very close.

In caring for me, my parents would look ahead and try to eliminate anything that might cause me discomfort. It was almost like walking ahead and clearing the path of someone without sight so that there is no chance of them tripping over any obstacles. My parents walked ahead of me and cleared my path. Everyone was very protective, and from my brothers' behaviour, it was apparent that a conversation had taken place at some point, the gist of which was that they were to watch out for me. But those conversations never included me.

Looking back, I suppose that it was much easier for them to take care of physical things than try to address my emotional needs. Emotional exchanges had not been their culture; neither of my parents had been raised that way. The society in which they grew up did not allow for such 'frivolities'; the circumstances of their lives demanded that they grew up quickly and contributed towards supporting their families and the raising of younger siblings. That was their responsibility; people were dependent on them. When they started a family of their own, they focused on providing for our needs, and so we were well-tended, well-nurtured and well-educated. They were exceptional parents, but I do not think that anything in their past had prepared them for the manner of my arrival, nor for any emotional needs that I might have.

A cry for help?

Mum and Dad never discussed my arm, other than in relation to medical treatment or, in my mother's case alone, spiritual healing. I was never asked about the challenges of growing up with a disability, and never asked how I felt. The unintentional result of this was that I felt very isolated, and for several years I struggled through periods of suffocating sadness, anger and self-doubt. What seemed like the moodiness of teenage years ran a little deeper.

Now that I am the parent of teenage daughters, I shudder to think about how difficult a child I must have been during those turbulent, uncommunicative years when I withdrew into myself. I exhibited behaviour that was unusual in some respects. Two instances stand out in my mind; once, when I was about 12 years old, I dislocated my right shoulder in school during practice for the long jump for inter-house sports day. I enjoyed athletics, and at the time I had a competitive streak which stemmed from an unhealthy desire to function just like, or better than, an 'able-bodied' person – this was my way of proving that I was capable. That afternoon, I was trying to better my previous distance and fell awkwardly. A sickening snap told me that something was wrong before the excruciating pain exploded through my right side.

I lay still for a moment; everything seemed to be in slow motion and I saw shades of greys pass before my eyes. With the help of my friends I got up, slowly. Not wanting to make a fuss, I assured everyone that I was all right and walked off the track clutching my arm to my side. Every step hurt dreadfully. My arm had become like lead and its weight was tearing at my shoulder. A distance of a few yards seemed like I was attempting to climb the roughest mountain.

The driver was waiting for me in the school car park, and so I went home. It was a typical weekday afternoon; my parents were away, my siblings were engaged in one activity or the other, and the rest of the household was occupied doing whatever they were doing that day. Holding my arm to my side, I slowly made my way up to my bedroom, alerting no one. Usually the cook would have had lunch ready, but I had taken a packed lunch to school that day as I was returning late. And so it was easy to make my way up to my bedroom without encountering anyone. Somehow, I got undressed and into bed. The pain was making me feel nauseous and feverish. My arm was burning hot and throbbing. Still I said nothing.

A few hours later, it was time for dinner and someone came to my door to get me. I mumbled something about not being hungry and they went away. A short time after, our house help came up to say I was required at the table. Again I said that I was not hungry. The next time someone else came to my door, I pretended to be asleep and they went away again. My mother was out of town and expected back very late that night, long after we had gone to bed, so I was able to get away with it. I still remember the agony of that night; it was a long night and it seemed as though the morning would never come.

The following morning, my baby sister, who was almost three years old, came looking for me as she did every morning. She found me huddled in a ball, crying, and immediately went to get my mum. When Mother arrived, she was horrified by what she saw. My arm was burning hot to the touch, almost three times its normal size and hanging in a strange position. Hours later, when all the drama of getting it seen to was over, she wanted to know why I had said nothing. Confusion was plastered across her face as she pressed me for an answer. The doctors had expressed great surprise that I had endured that level of pain in silence for so many hours. My response was a mumbled, 'I dunno.'

She could get nothing more out of me.

I still to this day have no answer. But I think that I had fallen into a pattern of silence, of dealing with challenges on my own.

A few years later, when I was about 14 or 15 years old, I was in hospital in Boston, Massachusetts having just undergone one in a series of surgeries. It was the day after the surgery and I was being seen by a raft of surgeons. One of them seemed to be more concerned with how my body was working, and I thought it odd that I was being asked questions about the regularity of my periods. When I told him that they were as regular as clockwork and had been since they started on my thirteenth birthday, he looked a little confused and said that it might be a good idea for me to have a chat with my mother, and that he would send her in.

Mother came in and was very upset that I had not told her when my periods had first started. Although I did not say so at the time, my first thought was, 'But you never said anything to me about periods and what to expect either!' We had never had 'the talk' and my life lesson was left to biology textbooks and the dodgy information from my more advanced friends! I was embarrassed and a little indignant to hear that both she and my father had discussed their concerns about my 'delayed development' and what might be causing it, and that he had suggested that she have a doctor give me a complete check-over when we were next in hospital. Hence the doctor's visit. Interestingly, no one had thought to ask me the simple question first. But this was typical of the way my family worked. The tendency was always to attempt to identify a solution to problems, and try to take care of immediate and anticipated issues. But I, on the other hand, wanted to be engaged: I was desperate for someone to ask me what I wanted and how I was feeling rather than trying to 'fix' a perceived problem. Even if I was unable to unravel and articulate my jumbled thoughts and emotions, I wanted to be consulted nonetheless. To this day I still react strongly when I feel decisions are being made concerning me without my input being sought.

These examples were some of the pointers that now as an adult I recognise as being indicative of some sort of cry for help. At the time I simply internalised everything. I did, however, make certain decisions. I decided that I would do whatever I could to ensure that my younger sisters did not experience some of the things that I did, and that they would always have someone to talk to. Much later on, I also developed an interest, which I trace back to my own childhood experiences, in young girls living with disabilities whose circumstances may not have been as positive as mine had been. In a way that I cannot explain, my path has crossed the paths of different young girls experiencing challenges of one form or another. Over time I have learned to share my own experiences, and I am always surprised by the impact that this simple act of vulnerability has had.

Looking beyond yourself

Many times the challenges that we face give us a deeper sensitivity towards, and a greater awareness of, others. We are better equipped to reach out in empathy to someone who is experiencing the same pain that we ourselves have experienced. I feel a strong pull towards disabled children struggling with the trials of adolescence because I lived through those struggles. Each time I looked in the mirror I did not like what I saw. It did not help that I was stick thin with a body that screamed 'ironing board' rather than 'cola bottle'! In my immature mind there was more about me that pointed to 'different' than to 'the same'. I was desperate to blend in, but instead I stood out.

I knew that I looked different in so far as my arm was different, and I had tried so desperately all my life to compensate for or overcome that difference. I had not realised just how much I tried to cover up my arm. Whenever I would meet people for the first time, I would place my arm behind me or in my pocket, or cover it up as often as I could. But this had not always been the case. I only became self-conscious in my teenage years. Prior to that, I was carefree and had no qualms. What this awareness did was open my eyes to be able to read the signs in other people. To notice things that perhaps others did not notice. Recently, I found myself conversing with a young girl whose leg had been severely weakened following a childhood illness. I remember saying to her, 'I'm sure you don't like summer that much.' She could not hide her surprise as she asked how I knew – I knew because I had been there. This girl would not wear shorts or skirts – nothing that would reveal her legs. I knew her frustrations and fears; I knew, because she could well have been me.

I remember seeing a young lady on a train once, who had some sort of disfigurement to the left side of her face. Anyone looking at her from the right side would be struck by her beauty; she had the most lustrous hair and flawless skin, but this only served to make her situation seem all the more like fate's wicked blow. I noticed how she sat, head tilted, looking out of the window. Using her hair to conceal the side of her face, constantly looking down, she would not meet anyone's gaze. As I looked at her, I wondered how this challenge affected her daily life and what kind of impact it had on her. I did not know anything about her, but I could safely conclude that she had encountered some challenges in her life which may have affected her ability to express her true self. Without knowing more about her, how she had responded and continues to respond to life would remain a mystery to me.

Parents and carers

I would like to take this opportunity to address a few words to the parents of children and adolescents living with a disability. There is the danger of focusing too much on a disabled child's apparent weaknesses. Parents may sometimes overlook the potential within that broken body, just waiting for the right person to release it through effort, encouragement and acceptance. Each child is an individual with their own uniqueness and it is important to view them as such. I strongly believe that within every child lies a reservoir of untapped potential just waiting to be realised. With love and encouragement, a child's personality and talents will gradually become apparent. It is a parent's responsibility to support and encourage their child, to love them as they are – this is not and should never be dependent on whether the child conforms to any definition of acceptability. Parents should cultivate what best-selling author Stephen Covey describes as 'internal sources of security' so that their feelings of worth are not defined by other people's opinions of what is normal or acceptable appearance or behaviour.[2] I am convinced that this security can only come from God.

As I have got older, I have tried to put myself in my parents' position – especially my mother; to understand the impact of raising a disabled child in our African culture. It was not that long ago when multiple-birth children in several African societies were thought of as evil and abandoned to certain death in forests. Nothing had prepared my parents for the challenge of raising a child with a disability. There must have been questions from strangers, family and friends alike. There must have been questions from both of them. Could they in some way have contributed to this? Could it have been prevented? Was it temporary; could it be fixed? Would I be accepted? How could they best support me? What sort of life would I have? What sort of future lay ahead? With maturity I now have a more sympathetic understanding of what they must have faced. There was no precedent for them upon which to draw. Their approach was to ensure that I lacked nothing that was in their power to provide. Perhaps they overcompensated with material things, but I was never in any doubt that I was loved, cherished beyond words and extremely special. Whatever mistakes they made were wholly inadvertent, and I cannot in good conscience judge them harshly. Their love gave me a security and confidence that is unshakeable, and in no small measure helped to shape me into the person that I am today.

Help for the journey

I have found this to be true, that God provides help for every part of the journey. When I look back over my life I see a long list of people who have encouraged and supported me and who have shown me that there is a way around every challenge. Some of them are particularly memorable because of the extent to which they impacted my life – people like my art teacher, Mr Broadhurst, who was a very fascinating and somewhat frightening character. He had the most unruly forest of brown, silver-tipped hair that looked like the bristles of an African broom. I was convinced that a comb that could tame his unshorn forest was yet to be invented. His hair was in keeping with his character, for there was something very unconventional and rebellious about him. He grunted more than he spoke. All the children called him 'Butch' behind his back. When I asked why, I was told that it had something to do with a resemblance to a bulldog.

Butch terrified me, and I was immediately tongue-tied in his presence. He was head of art, and he received the news that I was the latest addition to his sixth-form art class in what I soon learned was typical fashion for him; he simply peered at me over the top of his glasses, asked my name, and grunted. I would later learn that Butch did not stand on form and ceremony and that he had a heart of pure gold.

I had just arrived, with my second brother, Ikechi, at our boarding school in Cumbria, UK, which would be my home for the next three years. I was bewildered, very anxious and a little dazed by the overnight transformation in my environment. The little village in which the school was situated was as far removed from the more familiar London as east is from west, and my anxiety-ridden mind was incapable of producing a cord long enough to connect the two.

I had just spent the summer in hospital for yet another surgery, and began my first term at school in England complete with a plaster cast and two metal pins in my arm. My mother was to return to England in four weeks to take me back to Boston, Massachusetts, USA to have the cast removed. In the interim, and for the foreseeable future, I could not participate in any sporting activities. Butch thought it might be a good idea for me to spend the long afternoons in the art workshop rather than be cooped up in my House.

That was the beginning of a very interesting period which had such far-reaching consequences for me. Most afternoons there would be just a handful of us working on different projects. Butch would wander round to see what each person was doing, and to offer guidance. Some of the pupils were making different things out of clay and throwing pots on a potter's wheel, some were sculpting various objects, forging things out of metal, or drawing and painting. I loved spending time surveying other people's work. I was particularly fascinated by the potter's wheel and by the speed with which a lump of clay could be transformed into a beautiful piece simply by cupping your hands or by moving them up and down and pressing with your thumbs. I was desperate to try it out for myself, but knew that it was highly unlikely. Even if I was not constrained by the bulky plaster cast, the fingers of my right arm were clenched in a fist and I did not have much control over them. So inevitably, after watching for a while, I would walk away.

The workshop was dusty and a little chaotic, but it was home to me, and I looked forward to the afternoons three times a week when I spent two hours before teatime enveloped in a creative bubble. One day I arrived to find Butch hunched over the potter's wheel. I could not see what he was doing, and so I said hello and then began working on a vase that was an ongoing project. Several minutes later he called me over. I was intrigued by what I saw. He had fashioned a polystyrene glove-like contraption shaped like a block but curved and smooth at one end and hollowed out at the other end. He had his clenched right fist inserted into the hollow bit which he used as a support for the pot that he was throwing. It took a few minutes before I figured out what he was doing. Butch knew that I was desperate to try throwing a pot, but the cast on my hand prevented this. Also you generally 'needed' two hands. He had invented this polystyrene thing which was to act as a second hand, and over many hours he had experimented with it. It was quite amusing because Butch was right-handed and, as I am left-handed, he was trying to work with his left hand to simulate what it would be like for me. Such was his dedication. He showed me the pots that he had made with his invention. There were about a dozen different shapes, lined up to the side and telling a story. You could see the progression from the first misshapen blob to what was quite an attractive vessel.

Endless possibilities

In that moment it was all about possibilities, and I was bursting with excitement. Butch motioned to me to get on the wheel. He wrapped a black bin liner around my plaster-encased right arm, which he inserted into the 'glove'. I clambered on to the seat, and he slapped a small mound of clay in the centre of the wheel, grunting in satisfaction at his perfect hit.

'Throw some pots,' he said and disappeared around the corner.

A smile pulled on each side of my face. I began doing what I had seen Butch do, and what I had practised in my mind so many times before. I could not stop grinning. My first attempt resembled an alien from the deep. The next few were little better. I kept trying. The clay collapsed time after time. After about an hour of trying, I looked like I had got too friendly with a cement mixer, but there was a small pot spinning proudly in the centre of the wheel. Butch grunted when he came by to inspect my work.

'That's good, Chizor,' he said. 'Throw another one.'

I began again. I pressed and kneaded. Minutes ticked by. I squeezed and pulled. Another pot emerged. I was surprised to see how good it was. I wanted to scream and dance and shout all at once. It felt great. Two grunts signified Butch's approval. He ran a wire through the base of the pot, separating it from the wheel, and then transported it carefully to the drying room. Over the next few weeks the pot was glazed and fired. When its transformation was complete, it was displayed proudly. And it looked quite beautiful too. It was a symbol of my triumph, and for many years a wonderful reminder of the fact that life is packed full of endless possibilities.

That day Butch joined my list of those people who are placed in our lives to act as launch pads for the next phase. In the months following, I recorded many 'firsts' in his class which I attribute largely to his belief in me – he made me want to do more, and made me believe that I could do more.

At the end of the summer term, we were visited by Her Royal Highness, Anne, the Princess Royal in commemoration of the 400th anniversary of the school, and a plaque that I had made under Butch's guiding eye was selected by our headmaster as a gift for her from the entire school. That was an incredible experience for me and entirely unexpected, and it stands out as one of the most memorable events in my school career. I was awarded with school colours for art, and my name was added to the school's annals. Butch's delight at yet another success boosted my confidence no end. I have never forgotten his impact on my life, and I often pray that struggling young people have a Butch in their lives too.

---

[1] Alexander de Seversky was a pilot, inventor and businessman, amongst other things, who served in the Russian naval air service when World War One began. He lost his leg in a plane crash in 1915 and subsequently immigrated to the United States, where he formed an aviation company.

[2] Stephen R. Covey, *The 7 Habits of Highly Effective People: Powerful Lessons in Personal Change*. A Fireside book. (New York, Simon & Schuster, 1990). First Fireside edition.

Chapter four
Challenged, not disabled

Being born with a disability, can sometimes be a struggle, but
it is the ability to overcome such a challenge, that makes it so
worth the fight. NEVER GIVE UP!!!
(Robert M. Hensel, Guinness World Record holder[1])

I have come to regard disability more as a challenge (that is,
something difficult but which is capable of stimulating and
motivating) and less as an obstacle (something that hinders,
obstructs or interferes with progress) that rules out a person. I
see it as an opportunity to show the glory of God in one's life. I
think of the word 'disabled' as nothing more than a label, a
classification. For me, it is primarily a means of grouping people
depending on perceived common features. The fact that you
have been classed as disabled does not mean that you have to
see yourself in those terms.

'Specially constructed and fit for purpose'

I was always uncomfortable with words such as 'disabled' and
'handicapped', and even more so when I looked up synonyms
for these words. Words such as affliction, defect, disorder,

handicap, impairment, infirmity, malady, disqualification, impotency, inability, incapacity, incompetency, unfitness, and weakness jumped off the page as I stared. The negative connotation in each of these words was clear. It took me to a moment of deep reflection as I thought about how God Himself regards each of us. Genesis 1:31 tells us that after God created humanity, 'God looked over all he had made, and he saw that it was very good!' (NLT) The Lord did not then and has not since made any mistakes; it therefore follows that you are not a mistake of nature. I am not a mistake of nature. God did not lose control at the moment of my birth. Nothing takes Him by surprise. The Bible says that we are 'fearfully *and* wonderfully made' (Psalm 139:14, NKJV). I chewed over this phrase for a long time, dissecting it until I believed it. Now I think of myself as 'fearfully *and* wonderfully made' – in other words, 'specially constructed and fit for purpose'. I choose to think of myself this way. It is a choice which I have to reinforce regularly.

Strength in weakness

The Bible tells many stories of people who had various 'disabilities'. But interestingly, contrary to disqualifying them, it was the fact that they were 'disabled', weak or unfit in the eyes of society, that qualified them for the Lord's work. This is because it is in our weakness that His strength is revealed and emphasised. The apostle Paul said to the Corinthians:

> Three times I called upon the Lord *and* besought [Him] about this *and* begged that it might depart from me;
> But He said to me, My grace (My favor and loving-kindness and mercy) is enough for you [sufficient against any danger and enables you to bear the trouble manfully]; for *My* strength *and* power are made perfect (fulfilled and completed) and **show**

themselves most effective in [your] weakness. Therefore, I will all the more gladly glory in my weaknesses *and* infirmities, that the strength *and* power of Christ (the Messiah) may rest (yes, may pitch a tent over and dwell) upon me!

So for the sake of Christ, I am well pleased *and* take pleasure in infirmities, insults, hardships, persecutions, perplexities *and* distresses; for when I am weak [in human strength], then am I [truly] strong (able, powerful in divine strength).
(2 Corinthians 12:8–10, my emphasis)

The Message puts it this way:

At first I didn't think of it as a gift, and begged God to remove it. Three times I did that, and then he told me,
My grace is enough; it's all you need.
My strength comes into its own in your weakness.
Once I heard that, I was glad to let it happen. I quit focusing on the handicap and began appreciating the gift. It was a case of Christ's strength moving in on my weakness. Now I take limitations in stride, and with good cheer, these limitations that cut me down to size – abuse, accidents, opposition, bad breaks. I just let Christ take over! And so the weaker I get, the stronger I become.

We are not told what Paul's ailment was specifically; he makes reference to a 'thorn in [his] flesh',[2] but we do know that it caused him great discomfort. Though he wanted to be rid of it, he had come to the realisation that the power of God could be revealed more strongly in contrast to his weakness. Although it may seem somewhat extreme to 'gladly glory in … infirmities',[3] your circumstances are an opportunity for the Lord to use you to 'destroy the wisdom of the wise',[4] by showing how much can be accomplished through someone, in spite of apparent weaknesses.

So, if you are in that special category of 'weak' people, then declare from this moment that you are strong ('let the weak say,

I am strong'[5]), and that you can do all things through Christ who strengthens you. Begin to see your situation not as a disqualification but as a challenge. Whilst I may be physically challenged, I am certainly not dis-abled! Recently a lady used an expression that I like; she talked about her 'disabled' son as being 'differently abled'. I liked the phrase for one reason only: the fact that it pointed to abilities which, whilst they may not follow usual lines, were nonetheless present. In a sense, it conveys a positive message in implying that there are other ways of looking at or of doing things.

'Differently abled'

There are several examples of people who have excelled in their chosen fields notwithstanding the fact that they lived with physical challenges. Beethoven was deaf and yet his symphonies continue to bless the world; Stevie Wonder and Ray Charles, both blind, made immense contributions to the contemporary music industry. I continue to be inspired and challenged by such people, and by more ordinary, less famous people.

Many years ago I was intrigued by the story of a woman called Joni Eareckson Tada who became a quadriplegic following a freak accident when she was a teenager. Her positive outlook on life was amazing considering her circumstances. Rather than dwelling on the things she could not do, she set out new goals and challenges for herself. She learned how to paint with a brush held between her teeth, and over time became an accomplished artist. She also became a writer and an inspiration to countless people who had undergone similar tragedies and could identify with her experiences. As I read her story, I wondered where all this talent was prior to her accident? As is the case with many of us, it was lying untapped somewhere within her, and it took great adversity to bring it to the surface. Today she is happily married, a world-renowned advocate for people with disabilities, a broadcaster, an author of numerous books, and has received various awards and honours for her work.

I also saw news footage featuring two very different ladies. The elder was one of the thalidomide babies[6] of the 1960s. Her mother, like countless women during this period, had taken the drug thalidomide, which was heralded as a revolutionary cure for morning sickness in pregnancy. The effects were widely reported cases of extensive foetal abnormality, and the birth of numerous babies without limbs or with stumps and flippers instead of legs and arms. This lady, one of the more fortunate ones, was born without arms but with legs and feet. She went on to live a normal life, including having a baby of her own, whom she managed to care for with her feet. The picture of this lady changing her baby's nappies, feeding him, bathing him and carrying him with her feet and teeth was indelibly impressed upon my memory. I thought at the time, and still do, that I, with less of a challenge physically, have no excuse for giving up.

The other person, considerably younger, was an 11-year-old schoolgirl who lost her lower left limb in a bomb blast. I had followed her story at the time of the incident with interest, and wondered how she would adapt to her new life. Not long after the loss of her limb, it was reported in the local media that she had taken up swimming, and after only six months had beaten off the competition to secure a place on the national disabled swimming team for her country. At such a young age, she had displayed exceptional courage in turning adversity into something positive, and as a result, she has a future brimming with endless possibilities.

I also watched a rather amusing report of a woman who had lost her right leg in an accident; she sought the help of the local media to assist her in making contact with a lady she had met previously who also happened to have lost her left leg. They discovered that they had the same shoe size and decided that when they bought a pair of shoes, rather than simply discarding the unused shoe, they could each wear one shoe of the same pair!

When I think of all these wonderful people, what then is my excuse for not reaching for newer heights?

Is your glass half-full or half-empty?

When I reflect on disability, I see parallels with the 'half-full/half-empty' concept. A glass filled halfway with water may be described either as half-full or half-empty, depending on who is describing it and how that person sees it. The key lies in how one sees oneself. Are you 'challenged' as opposed to 'disabled'? Is life half-empty because you have lost the use of your legs, or half-full because there is so much you can do with your hands? Although a limitation is one of the least expected places from which creativity emerges, a physical disability can often be a trigger for creativity.

I remember that I was always improvising when I was young; a child's mind is a wellspring of creativity. I loved to skip and was quite good at it, but I needed someone else to turn the rope. One day, there was no one to play with, and I wanted to skip. After a few unsuccessful attempts – I could not lift my right arm above my head – my eyes rested on the metal handle of a gate in our play area. I thought that it just might work as a second hand. I tied one end of the rope to the handle, stretched it out and began turning. To my delight it seemed to be working. I got a rhythm going and counted down in my head.

'Three, two, one.'

I jumped in. It worked perfectly!

On the first try I counted four skips, and then six. At the end of the first day I could jump in and out with ease, and lost track of the number of skips I had managed before collapsing in a giggling heap, excited by my latest discovery.

So many people faced with disabilities of one form or another have gone on to develop skills or discover talents that had been previously hidden. Your imagination is stretched and you begin to think about ways in which you can get around a limitation. In my own life, the result has surprised me. You really have no idea what you can do until you try.

I remember reading about a remarkable lady called Alison Lapper and the controversy that brought her media attention, but which also highlighted the amazing creativity of the human spirit. Ms Lapper was born with phocomelia, or limb deformity, which is a congenital condition characterised by the absence of limbs, similar to that experienced by thalidomide victims. She was born with no arms and extremely shortened legs. Her life was one of proving people wrong. When she was born she was not expected to live at all, or if she did, to be no more than a 'cabbage' in a wheelchair. It was believed that she would be institutionalised all her life, with no potential. Aged only 17 years, she left the institution where she was raised, in search of independence. Ms Lapper went on to study art and was awarded a first class honours degree. She became an accomplished artist, painting with brushes held between her teeth, and subsequently became a member of the Association of Mouth and Foot Painting Artists of the World.[7] She was later conferred with an MBE for services to art.[8]

I first learned of her at the height of the controversial debate surrounding the choice of a nude statue of her heavily pregnant form for the fourth plinth at the famous landmark in Trafalgar Square in central London. For some time, arguments flew back and forth. Some people thought the statue was inappropriate, situated alongside Nelson's Column and King George IV, and others thought it reflected a positive advance in society's treatment of the disabled person. Notwithstanding the furore, the statue remained in place for 18 months, and seven years later a 43-foot version graced the opening ceremony of the 2012 Paralympic Games in London. Alison's story is a compelling testimony of one person's sheer determination and desire to break boundaries and to embrace a full life, in spite of the physical and social barriers that were a fact of her daily existence.

> Learning to be creative within the confines of our limitations is the best hope we have to transform ourselves and collectively transform our world.
> Phil Hansen, American multimedia artist
> (From a TED Talk entitled 'Embrace the Shake')[9]

---

[1] Robert Hensel is, amongst other things, a poet-writer with over 900 publications. Born with spina bifida, he holds the Guinness World Record for the longest non-stop wheelie in a wheelchair, which covered a distance of 6.178 miles. He is also an advocate for disability rights for disabled Americans.

[2] See 2 Corinthians 12:7, NLT.

[3] 2 Corinthians 12:8–9.

[4] 1 Corinthians 1:19, NLT.

[5] Joel 3:10.

[6] Thalidomide was hailed as a wonder drug when it was first introduced as a sedative in 1956 in Europe. It was found to be particularly effective in pregnancy to combat some of the symptoms of morning sickness and was specifically marketed to be used during pregnancy. However, the drug had catastrophic consequences for the developing foetus. Unknown to its manufacturers and researchers, the thalidomide molecules breached the wall of the placenta with devastating effects on the unborn child. It resulted in death to babies, and for those surviving, a vast range of malformations including deafness, blindness, limb deformities, cleft

palate and internal defects. Thalidomide was marketed in approximately 46 countries under different names. It was withdrawn from the market in 1961 in Germany where it first emerged, although it continued to be available in some countries until 1962. The full extent of the numbers affected by the drug worldwide is unknown; however, it is thought that thousands of babies were born disabled as a result. The tragedy caused by thalidomide changed the way new drugs are evaluated for use in people.

[7] The Association of Mouth and Foot Painting Artists of the World has its origins in 1956, when eight disabled European artists got together to form a self-help association in Britain, allowing them to maintain economic independence by marketing their work which is sold as greetings cards, calendars, illustrated books, and prints. The movement has attained worldwide exposure.

[8] The Member of the Most Excellent Order of the British Empire (MBE) award is classed amongst the Order of the British Empire. It is the most junior in the British and Commonwealth honours system. Dating back to June 1917, it was established by King George V, and recognises individuals who have contributed significantly to public life or made outstanding achievements in a particular field.

[9] https://www.ted.com/talks/phil_hansen_embrace_the_shake (accessed 30th September 2015).

Chapter five
Whose opinion matters?

Treat a man as he is and he will remain as he is. Treat a man
as he can and should be and he will become as he can and
should be.
(Stephen R. Covey[1])

More often than not, one's life mirrors one's childhood
circumstances; so an adult that exudes confidence in the majority
of cases had a childhood filled with possibilities and hope.
Conversely, a child surrounded with impossibilities often grows
into an adult lacking in confidence and self-esteem. Through
countless influences, which may include those from parents,
school, television, and other forms of media, we develop habits
and thought patterns that are often in direct contradiction with
the Word of God. In many cases, we have been conditioned by
society to see physical challenges as limitations or as obstacles to
us attaining our goals.

Very often there appears to be the assumption that one's
goals need to be lowered because one has some sort of disability;
there will never be a shortage of people who will tell you how
far you can or ought to go. The painful thing is that sometimes
these people may be close to you; they may have good intentions
and will tell you that they have your best interests at heart and
do not want to see you get hurt. For those of us who live with

various challenges, it may sometimes be easier to accept this view of ourselves because it means that we have an excuse for not trying, or for giving up if we do not immediately succeed at something. As a result, we become a victim of the opinions of others.

I was never short of encouragement whilst I was growing up, because the hands that shaped me were very gentle hands, but there came a time when I had to leave the security of my family and home and make my way in the world like everyone else, among people who would have an opinion about what I could or could not do, people who would make judgements on the basis of these opinions, and people who would not be willing to give me a chance.

I remember the first time I was refused a job because it was felt that I could not cope physically. I remember the hurt and pain, which after the initial period of self-pity gave way to a steely determination to prove 'them' wrong. I remember thinking in frustration, 'Yes, my arm may not work as quickly or as well as someone else's, but there is nothing wrong with my brain!' I have encountered several similar incidents in the years since and I am sure I will still encounter others in the years to come. *You cannot change the way the world chooses to look at you, or the opinions that are formed about you, but you can change the way you respond to incidents such as these.* Your response is within your control.

Whose voice are you listening to?

How do you see yourself? In the majority of cases, the opinions we form of ourselves are based on what we have been told about ourselves or the experiences we have had in our formative years. Whatever these may be, whether for good or for bad, it is extremely difficult to erase words from one's childhood. I was blessed in that I had an upbringing filled with encouragement and much love. I grew up knowing that I had a lot to offer. Like any child, I made plans about what I would become. I had countless dreams, each one bigger than the former, and I gave great thought to my future. My talents were encouraged and my successes, no matter how seemingly insignificant, were celebrated at home. I had no doubt that my parents were proud of me. If they had any concerns about my future, they never expressed them to me. At home, I felt safe and secure. I did not hope I would get married; I *knew* I would get married, and I knew I would have children.

I emphasise this point about marriage because in the African culture, marriage is of extreme importance and there is a social stigma attached to being of marriageable age and remaining unmarried. Even now, in more enlightened times, you can almost sense the relief as families give away their daughters in marriage. The pressure is doubled if you have a disabled daughter. Unspoken or not, the fear is that 'no one will marry her'. There was a terrible practice across some African societies, which fed this fear and fostered an environment of prejudice.

During traditional marriage ceremonies, the families of the grooms often publicly count the fingers and toes of the bride before payment of the bride price or dowry, as a means of ensuring that they are not getting 'damaged goods'. Although this practice has lost significance over the years, the underlying view is that disability is something that is best hidden. For the majority, disability equates to a future devoid of hope and value. Widespread poverty only serves to exacerbate this imbalance. As a child growing up, I was struck by the fact that there were no disabled role models, people who were successes in their chosen fields and living examples of the truth that one can have a fulfilled and normal life, notwithstanding their physical challenges.

There were two categories of disabled people that I saw: the first were pupils of two schools for the blind (and partially sighted) and the deaf (and hearing impaired) in the city where I grew up – both schools were featured a few times on television programmes during occasions such as Children's Day and Independence Day. The children would feature in debates, drama, and dance, or play musical instruments. I remember that they were always so well turned-out; the white of their blouses and shirts really shone, and the girls had big bows in their hair. It was clear that someone was determined to ensure that they had a chance in life, and both schools were doing a laudable work. But they seemed to be a spectacle, and the few times that we saw them walking on the streets around their school there was always a small crowd of people pointing and staring at them. They were being raised in a sheltered environment, but I have no idea what became of the children after they left the safe confines of their school.

Curiously, I never once saw any disabled adults in mainstream society. The only disabled adults that I saw, the second category to which I was exposed, were street beggars who eked out a meagre living by begging in public places. Their plight was pitiful, and their future appeared to be as permanent as set concrete, with no prospect of change. They were on the streets of the city, displaying terrible deformities which they hoped would elicit sympathy from commuters. As soon as the traffic slowed they converged on the cars, jostling for prime position, with pleading eyes, hand gestures and sing-song voices conveying their dire need. It was horrendous to see, and it bothered me immensely. Their situation was a feasible explanation for the aggression that they sometimes displayed.

They were regarded as a menace to society. In truth, they were a terrible indictment on a country that had such extensive natural resources.

Even for families that were economically stable, the arrival of a disabled child posed serious problems. Superstition and culture fed the misguided belief that disability was bad and there had to be a reason for it. It was either as a result of some evil perpetrated upon the family by a cruel third party, often envious friends or family members, or it was judgement for some offence committed by the family into which the child had come. It brought shame and was definitely a thing to be hidden away. The segregation was clear.

For years this one question has weighed heavily on my mind; why were there no visible disabled lawyers, broadcasters, politicians, teachers, doctors, and other professionals? It could not be that in a country the size of Nigeria there were no disabled people; in fact, the opposite was the case. Poor medical care and facilities, a high occurrence of road traffic accidents and war are factors that contribute to disability in developing countries.

It was evident that there were scores of disabled people living in the country, but then the nagging question that I never could answer related to the quality of life that these people had. Their fight was two-fold; it was a fight for physical survival and recognition on the one hand, and opportunity on the other. If you were disabled and economically strapped (and they tended to go hand in hand), then you were greatly disadvantaged. If you were disabled and female, then your chances in life were extremely bleak. You were vulnerable, marginalised, and at great risk.

Aside from the visible physical challenges, there is also the emotional trauma to be grappled with. I recall a conversation I had with a girl I had known for several years. We first met when we attended the same secondary school. She was disabled as a result of contracting polio in early childhood. We were friendly in the manner that schoolmates often are during our schooldays, but lost touch in subsequent years. I had regained contact with her eight years after we left school, and for a while we remained in close contact, catching up on our lives. Even though we were not particularly close whilst at school, I now found myself drawn to her. I was struck by her low opinion of herself and by her lack of enthusiasm about the future. During that period, I had just passed my driving test and was buoyed by this victory and the implications of my newly discovered independence. I remember telling her that she too could easily begin to drive a car with the proper modifications to suit her specific needs. But I seemed to be unable to infect her with my excitement. She was unenthusiastic and appeared completely closed off to the idea.

Inevitably, our conversation turned to relationships and marriage. She expressed the fear that her younger sisters would get married and she would be left 'on the shelf'. After much probing, she said she did not rate her chances of getting married. I probed further.

'Why do you think that?' I asked curiously.

I looked at her. I saw a pretty girl with no self-belief and a certain sadness about her. It turned out that her mother had said (often in tears) several times while she was growing up, 'My poor daughter, who will marry you?'

I can only imagine what that must have done to her self-esteem. She had grown up thinking that she had nothing to offer, and that anyone who showed an interest in her was doing her a favour. When she was older, she was so grateful for any attention from young men that she was prepared to do anything against her better judgement in a bid to keep their interest. She made some poor choices and, disgracefully, some of these young men exploited her. Thinking about it now, even after so long, still causes my hackles to rise. I remember saying to her at the time that she had a lot to offer, that I had a lot to offer, and that anyone who thought otherwise was shallow and undeserving of either of us. I told her I was so sure I would marry a wonderful person who would love me just as I am, but I could not convince her; as she rightly pointed out, there was 'no evidence at this time to back my claim' – I had no boyfriend, and my husband was very much in the future. I walked away from that meeting feeling so sad that I had been unable to paint a picture of a brighter future.

On my wedding day, years later, I sat at my dresser in a quiet moment before the activities kicked in. I peered at my reflection in the mirror. Behind me, the little gems stitched across my dress sparkled in the early morning sunlight, catching my eye. Quite unexpectedly my thoughts turned to her, and I wished I could have told her that it is possible after all, but by then we had again lost contact with one another. I still think about her, usually at milestone events in my life, and I wonder where she is and what has become of her.

You can choose

Every adverse situation can either destroy you or mould you into something or someone positive. You can choose to be bound by events and opinions from the past, or you can fight against everything negative. At the outset, I do not think that I made a conscious choice or decision; I just rebelled against the injustice of any limitations based on an occurrence over which I had no control. My sense of right and wrong, which was largely shaped by my parents, told me that discrimination of any form was wrong and not to be tolerated. As a child, my constant refrain was 'that's not fair', and I would fight with everything I had to ensure that the balance of fairness was restored. As I grew older and ventured out into the world, I soon realised that making choices is a lifelong exercise. From then on, I exercised my right and responsibility to choose.

I choose to have a fighting spirit, to challenge any limitations placed on me. I choose to extend my boundaries on a regular basis and aim for higher and higher marks; and I know that when I fall, and even if I do so several times, with the Lord's help I will dust myself down and try again. Day after day I face challenges that cause me to revisit my choices and demand a response from me. Life asks me questions like, 'What are you going to do, Chizor? How are you going to respond? What can you take away from this or that situation? What are you going to believe about yourself? Whose opinion really matters most?'

God's opinion settles all arguments

I have reached the conclusion that the only opinion that is always valid and which should settle all arguments is God's opinion, for the simple fact that it is the ultimate truth. He placed His seal of approval on you and I by declaring us to be 'very good' (Genesis 1:31). God's opinion is the only reliable opinion, the only one that you can truly trust AT ALL TIMES. His viewpoint is contrary to that of the world. He is a God of paradoxes. The world tends to make judgements based on the outward appearance, but God looks beyond to what lies within; the world rejects weakness, whilst God embraces weaknesses. The very attributes that would rule out you and I in the world's reckoning are of great value to Him. As I write, I think of biblical characters such as Moses, Gideon, and David who faced adversity in various forms.

I love Moses' story; I find myself returning to it time and again, perhaps because I identify with him in some respects. Whenever I read his story, I am struck by the contrast between his opinion of himself and God's opinion of him. He was overwhelmed by the size of the task that God had set before him. As we often do, he focused only on the things that made him incapable of succeeding. He said to God: 'Lord, I am not eloquent or a man of words, neither before nor since You have spoken to Your servant; for I am *slow of speech* and have a *heavy and awkward* tongue' (Exodus 4:10, my italics).

It is clear that he is lacking in confidence, possibly very self-conscious as a result of this speech impediment which is described as a 'slowness of speech'. And Moses was insecure. His insecurity was probably heightened by the fact that he had just spent 40 years in exile! I imagine that he only had sheep and his thoughts for company. Neither would have been of much use to him. The sheep could not talk to him at all, and his thoughts were probably talking too much, playing back to him all the reasons why he did not match up, and why he was of little use. I love the fact that God chose him in spite of his 'flaws', from amongst a multitude, to lead His people out of Egypt. God's response to him was that as he went in obedience to His command, He (the Lord) would be his mouth. But Moses was required to take the initial step.

I have experienced God's strength enabling me to do things that in myself I am incapable of doing when I take that first step. That first step is crucial. Sometimes it is as little as making one adjustment, or it might be a willingness to do something that terrifies you. No matter what that first step is for you, it signifies a trust in God. It is acknowledging that you are safe in His hands. I have never been disappointed by that first step. Whenever I look back, which I do often, and with the benefit of hindsight, I am always amazed as to what has followed.

I also love Gideon's story. There is something so credible about where we find him, hiding away in such a fearful state. It is almost laughable when the Angel of the Lord calls him a 'mighty man of valor' (Judges 6:12, NKJV). Just like we often are, Gideon is sceptical. His response went something like this: 'Er, God, I don't mean to be rude, but have You forgotten who I am? Just in case You don't know, I am Gideon. My tribe is the weakest, my family is the weakest family in the weakest tribe and amongst my siblings, I am the least of the sons in the weakest family in the weakest tribe!'

He asks God to confirm what He has said by showing him a series of signs. Ever so patiently God complies with his request. Gideon was not feeling very brave at the time; in fact, he was terrified, trying to thresh corn by stealth in the hope that he would not be discovered by the marauding Midian army which had oppressed his people for several years. When the Angel first appears to Gideon he says: 'The Lord *is* with you, you mighty man of valor!' (Judges 6:12, NKJV)

I think that the key to Gideon's eventual success was God's presence. With God there with him, guiding and directing him, he was able to achieve what he could never have achieved on his own. It is interesting and very encouraging to learn that much later on in the book of Hebrews, Gideon is described as a man of faith (Hebrews 11:32–34)!

God looked at stuttering Moses and saw a great orator; He looked at cowering Gideon and saw a valiant warrior. God Himself is the difference between our present reality and the limitless possibilities in our future.

How about letting God be your eyes, hands, ears, or legs? How about letting Him guide you and see how far you can go with His help?

If it is difficult to see yourself as being able to do much, consider this thought instead. The fact that you are achieving great things despite your challenges will encourage countless people, disabled or not, to aim for greater heights. People who come into contact with you will begin to ask themselves: 'What, then, is my excuse for not trying?' They will also wonder about the source of your strength and optimism. In that moment you will have an opportunity to speak of the impact Christ has had on your life and situation.

'Of course you can't, but I can!'

I recall one occasion when I was faced with something particularly daunting. I muttered repeatedly, 'Lord, I can't do this, I can't.' I sensed Him in my heart reply, 'Of course you can't, but I can!'

It dawned on me then that in myself, I can do nothing. However, the key to my success is in realising that *I am not in myself, I am in Him (Christ)* and am thus well equipped to face life's trials. You cannot build a successful life on negative thinking. Lies are the basis of every negative thing in our lives. The Bible refers to Satan as the father of all lies and all that is false;[2] and when we doubt God's Word, we automatically believe Satan's word (lies). It is impossible to do both. Once I realised this, I began to cultivate a new attitude. I now face each new challenge with the awareness that with God's help I will come through. 'I can do all things through Christ who strengthens me' (Philippians 4:13, NKJV).

I really believe this, and it has spurred me on to attempt new things and sometimes to go back and re-attempt things that I may have 'failed' at first time round.

As you try new things, there will be many failed attempts and many times when you will feel as though it is impossible. The key is to never give up trying and to understand that there is more than one way of achieving something; two essential traits are perseverance and patience. There are many stories of sprinters who have no legs, writers who have no arms, artists who paint with their teeth, and a host of others. Eleanor Roosevelt wrote in her autobiography about her husband, Franklin Delano Roosevelt, the thirty-second President of the United States of America, who served an unprecedented four terms in office and who was disabled after contracting polio at age 39 years:

> Franklin's illness proved a blessing in disguise, for it gave him strength and courage he had not had before. He had to think out the fundamentals of living and learn the greatest of all lessons-infinite patience and never-ending persistence.[3]

---

[1] Stephen R. Covey, *The 7 Habits of Highly Effective People: Powerful Lessons in Personal Change.* A Fireside book. (New York, Simon & Schuster, 1990). First Fireside edition.

[2] John 8:44.

[3] Eleanor Roosevelt, from her autobiography: *The Autobiography of Eleanor Roosevelt* (Boston, MA: Da Capo Press) 1992. Also documented by Russell Freedman, *Eleanor Roosevelt: A Life of Discovery* (New York: Clarion Books, 1993) p.74.

Chapter six
The prison of your mind

Men are not prisoners of fate, but only prisoners of their own
minds.
(Franklin D. Roosevelt, US President, 1882–1945[1])

I love fashion – I always have. I find elegant, tasteful clothes very
appealing, and I feel very good when I know I look good.
However, in the past I was never truly able to enjoy my love for
clothes or to fully express my flair for fashion. My wardrobe was
limited to clothes that covered up my body. I was more
comfortable during the winter months because warm clothing
meant covered arms. Each year as summer approached, my
thoughts were of those beautiful dresses, T-shirts and blouses
that I would never wear in public.

In the past, I only ever exposed my arms around family
members and very close friends. I have lost count of the number
of times that I refused to buy dresses or tops that I loved, simply
because they were short-sleeved or sleeveless. I was imprisoned,
held captive, prevented from revealing the true me.

I remember that I had my wedding dress modified to
something with which I was comfortable. I was panic stricken at
the thought that for one entire day I would have the eyes of close

to 1,000 people on me for extended periods. I felt awkward and ill at ease; my excitement was tempered by my nervousness, and the day seemed more like an ordeal rather than an opportunity to bask in the attention of so many.

Early on in our marriage, after watching me on several occasions during shopping trips when I would stop by certain clothes that I obviously liked, look at them for long periods and then buy something that was an obvious poor second choice, my husband, Bajo, decided to say something.

'Why don't you buy that, baby?' he said, pointing at a very pretty dress.

'Because it's got no sleeves,' my voice was short, coated heavily with irritation.

'So what?' he said, his eyes registering the awareness that he was missing something, but not sure what that might be.

I remember glaring at him, and not speaking to him for the rest of the day. I thought he was insensitive and cruel and told him so. He was completely confused by the short exchange. His attempts to elicit an explanation were thwarted by a wall of silence. Eventually he retreated to regroup. Even though we had never had a conversation around the issue, I just expected him to know. This was not rational, but then an emotional outburst seldom is.

Much later on, he coaxed me into articulating how I was feeling. For the first time in my life, I expressed my abhorrence of anything that resembled pity. I told him how I hate to see the look on people's faces turn from shock to pity and then to curiosity as they try unsuccessfully not to stare. The less tactful often ask, 'What happened to your arm?' The majority only question with their eyes. I always found these encounters painful and emotionally draining, and went out of my way to avoid them; hence the compulsion to cover up my arms whenever I was amongst strangers. All of this had translated into behaviour that was not me, behaviour which included shopping within such rigid boundaries.

I do not doubt that there were times when I have imagined these stares, but the point is that I had formed an opinion in my mind that this would be the inevitable outcome of every first encounter I had, and so my response was to avoid placing myself in potential situations. I deliberately speak in past tense because I am in a process of renewal with the help of the Lord. It is a slow process, but I reward myself for every step forward and try to arrest every step back. Bajo and I celebrate every little step as a major victory. This process of renewal began as I got closer to Jesus. The more my desire to know Him increased, the more I studied the Bible and the more questions I asked of Him. In our exchanges, I began to experience a greater sense of esteem and value.

How about me?

The process was not without its challenges. My heart was crying out for the freedom to express myself fully and without constraint, but my mind appeared to be working contrary to this desire. I thought that I could only be my real self without the burden of a disability to cope with. But the disability was my reality, and I had to be myself in spite of it. I was well aware that I could no longer have 'if onlys' as part of my vocabulary. I remember one day during a healing service at the church to which I belong, when I was feeling particularly weighed down. I had heard countless testimonies of other people being healed and quite frankly, I was fed up; fed up with people who constantly said that it was God's will to heal every ailment but never had a response as to why some people (and I fell into that

84

group) were not getting healed; fed up with having my hopes built up and then having them come crashing down. Most especially I was fed up with people who suggested that it was simply a question of faith, and that healing always followed whenever Jesus found faith that was strong enough. The implication was that if you were not healed then your faith was not strong enough, and perhaps you should look to building up your faith.

On that particular morning my heart was crying out, 'How about me, Lord? When will it be my turn?' His answer jolted me. Perhaps because I was not really expecting a response, and also because the response that came did not seem to answer my questions. I distinctly heard Him speak these words to my heart, 'You are not a mistake, I do not make mistakes. You are beautiful; never be ashamed of how you look.'

I have tried since then to see myself as God sees me, to stop hiding myself from the stares of the world, real and imagined; I constantly meditate on the following scriptures and find that I am increasingly gaining the strength to change my perspective. I realise that strongholds exist in the mind and I am determined, with the Lord's help, to rid myself of this torment.

The Lord *sets free the prisoners*,
    The Lord opens the eyes of the blind, the Lord lifts up those who are bowed down.
(Psalms 146:7–8, my italics)

For I know the thoughts *and* plans that I have for you, says the Lord, thoughts *and* plans for welfare *and* peace and not for evil, to give you hope in your final outcome.
(Jeremiah 29:11)

> I will be found by you, says the Lord, and I will release you from captivity …
> (Jeremiah 29:14)

When I first read these words, I thought of the children of Israel and their 400-year captivity in Egypt. Their story brought home to me the realisation that captivity far surpasses a physical imprisonment. Often, even after the physical prison has been dealt with, there is still the mindset that needs to be addressed. The latter is usually more problematic.

Consider the Israelites as an illustration. The Lord delivered them, through Moses, with many signs and wonders, and yet time and time again we see them giving in to doubt and mistrust. Why? Because in their minds and their psyche, they were still slaves in Egypt. All the stories that had been handed down through the generations were of slavery and bondage. None of God's promises carried enough weight, and they were incapable of embracing and walking in the knowledge that they had been set free. Until Joshua and Caleb, that is. They alone had the courage to reach for what had until then been a promise, and to turn it into reality.[2] The same 'courage' is being asked of us; we have been promised much, but the question is always whether we will have the courage to take the first step in ensuring that our potential is actualised.

I am truly convinced that the Lord has released me from captivity. I do not doubt my worth in His eyes. The difficult bit is walking into freedom. For me, this was to begin shopping with a different attitude. Now I indulge my sense of taste and style without constraint. I no longer look at clothes which I find attractive and then walk away. I buy what I like and I wear them too! When people have commented at the obvious changes I have replied with a coy smile, 'Watch this space! The real Chizor is about to be revealed!'

It is exciting and uncomfortable at the same time, but I am determined to take hold of my freedom with both hands. With the Lord's help, I will begin to embrace the summer months and the rest of my life without misgivings.

What do you see?

I realise that I must first visualise the possibilities in my future before I can attain them. The mind is a force that affects everything in one's future. The Lord spoke to my heart; I felt Him say, 'Chizor, what do you see? If you can see the invisible, you can do the impossible.' I pose this question to you: 'What do you see?'

What we see has a lot to do with what we experience and what we were told in our formative years. Words can build lasting pictures in our minds. When my schoolmate's mother said, 'Who will marry you?' she was in effect saying, 'You are not "marriage material"; it is very unlikely that anyone will want you because of the way you are.' Those words formed a picture in her mind which she was incapable of shifting when she became an adult. In contrast, there was never any attention drawn to my disability at home, and the expectation was that I would grow up and become whatever it was that I had set my heart on. My first picture was formed by parents whose message to me was: 'Dream big. You can be anything. You can do anything.'

Helping someone to dream

After completing my law degrees in England, I returned to Nigeria to attend the Nigerian Law School in preparation for the

Bar examinations. I spent about 18 months at the Law School, and during that time I got to meet all sorts of people from varied backgrounds. One was a middle-aged gentleman who worked in the school's main office as a messenger. He was modestly educated and struggling to provide for his burgeoning family. I met him when I went to complete my registration and pay the school fees. He liked the fact that my friends and I were polite and respected his office, and was pleasant in return.

As time went on, we enjoyed the perks of his office; he would always make sure that we did not have to wait for hours on end before someone attended to us whenever we went into the office. One day he told me that he had a 13-year-old daughter who, in his words, had a 'useless leg'; she had been born with one leg considerably shorter than the other and walked with great difficulty. There were additional health issues as a result, which he tried to articulate. He struggled to make ends meet and had several mouths to feed, the products of three wives. He was of the class and background that held the view that it was more beneficial to educate sons and not daughters, as girls would only get married and start producing babies and any investment would, in a sense, be lost. He felt that his daughter's situation was compounded because her marriage prospects could not be rated highly in view of her disability, and there seemed even less of a reason to continue to 'waste money' in educating her. He had resigned himself to the fact that she would be a burden for the rest of her life, and concluded that her siblings would have to look after her. It never entered his mind that she could actually make a living and look after herself. Interestingly he said that she was doing well at school – in fact, she was the brightest of all his children – but he still questioned the wisdom in keeping her on rather than concentrating on his other children. This was a source of contention with the girl's mother, who was a petty trader, a small-scale merchant hawking items of garden produce and cooked food to commuters from a makeshift booth at various bus terminals in the city, and who spent every penny that she made towards giving her child a start in life.

Unknown to me, he had been watching me since he had noticed my arm and was coming round to the thinking that perhaps it might be worthwhile to continue to educate her, if there was a chance that she could become something. But he still struggled with the stigma associated with disability, and because of the prejudices of his community, his mind could not grasp the possibility of a future life for her that included marriage and a family. He said that even if she were to find a suitor who was prepared to marry her, the man's family would never agree to such a union. I was surprised by his admission that if the situation was reversed and his son asked him to approach the family of a disabled girl with a marriage proposal on his behalf, he doubted that he would be willing to do so. Although he openly expressed the depth of his feelings, his struggle was clearly visible. He wanted the best for his child, but he was labouring under the burden of limited resources and the weight of societal prejudices.

He listened carefully as I told him that she could be anything with the right support and encouragement, and afterwards asked if he could bring her to see me. I did not know what I would say to her, but I agreed to the meeting. A few days later he walked up to me in the car park with his daughter in tow, mumbled something about some work that needed his urgent attention, and left her with me. She smiled shyly, saying nothing. I attempted to draw her out. She was a beautiful child, and within a few moments it was apparent that she was also quite intelligent. It was obvious that she had not had an easy time in her short life, for her eyes reflected the intensity of her experiences, but there was a determination about her, an unspoken refusal to accept the limitations placed on her by her situation and the prejudices of her community. When I asked her what she would like to be when she grew up, she looked down at her feet for a few moments.

'Before, I wanted to be a teacher, but Papa told me about you and that you can do everything, even driving. Now, I want to be a lawyer... like you,' she added, a little hesitantly.

I was taken aback. It was humbling and frightening to think that someone that I just met was inspired by the little that they could see of my life. I never envisaged myself as a role model, and I did not quite know how to respond.

'You can be anything you want to be,' I said quietly.

She smiled again.

I knew that the cards that she had been dealt were stacked against her, but I also knew that anything was possible and that she really could be her family's success story. I wondered how I could help her.

That moment stands out in my memory as one of the most meaningful periods during my stint at the law school. In me this young girl saw possibilities beyond the boundaries of her circumstances. If she realised this dream, she would be the first in her family to have completed secondary school and subsequently university. I was drawn to her, and almost immediately I began to contribute towards her education. At regular intervals I would pay her school fees, pay for her uniform and books. It was not a huge amount, but it made a difference. Her father struggled to express the depth of his gratitude, but I think that the bigger impact was in the change that was brought about in his thinking. He was affected by my life and my willingness to be involved in his child's life, and he began to question the prejudices around disability.

I believe that it was the Lord that caused our paths to cross at what was a critical stage in her life. The awareness that He had used me to touch a young, struggling girl, and to give her a better picture of her future, was very humbling and I considered it a tremendous privilege.

Can you see the 'unseen'?

Recently I was speaking to a wonderful lady who is presently living with multiple sclerosis. She said to me: 'This might sound strange, but recently I have had visions where I see myself running. In my dreams I am running.'

'So be it,' I said, smiling.

There was nothing strange about what she said and I understood perfectly. Can you 'see what cannot be seen'? Do you have a picture of your healing coming to pass? Do you see yourself successful, healthy, and joyful? Whatever your prison may be, you have got to be determined about releasing its hold over you. Begin to build a good picture of yourself. If you give up and cave in in your mind, it will happen in reality. If you think it will never happen for you, it will never happen for you; if you think good things will never happen to you, they never will.

Consider this little truth: *when you are down, you are the one who suffers most.*

All of the important battles we face will be waged within ourselves. Nothing great has ever been achieved except by those who dared believe that God was superior to any circumstance.[3]

---

[1] Franklin D. Roosevelt, 'Address to the Pan American Union, April 14 1939', (Page 44 Paper XIII – Address to the Governing Board of the Pan American Union, Washington DC, April 14 1939 – http://www.ibiblio.org/pha/7-2-188/188-13.html (accessed 21st September 2015).

[2] Numbers 13:26–30.

[3] John L. Mason, *You're Born an Original, Don't Die a Copy!* (Tulsa, OK: Insight International, 1993) p.37 Nugget #13.

Chapter seven
Why am I not healed, Lord?

Jesus answered, It was not that this man or his parents
sinned, but he was born blind in order that the workings of
God should be manifested (displayed and illustrated) in him.
(John 9:3)

From my earliest memories, the subject of healing has confused
me and often made me very uncomfortable. I grew up in a
Christian home, and my mother insisted that my siblings and I
attended church and Sunday school regularly. Whenever she
could not take us personally, we were carted off regardless of our
protests by our nanny. We all grew up very familiar with the
stories about Jesus' healing ministry in the Gospels. My mother
always said that one day, Jesus would heal me. She believed it
entirely and spoke to me about it often.

In search of healing

My entire childhood was filled with dreams and thoughts of that
wonderful day when Jesus would 'make my right arm just like
the other one'. I could not figure out how He would do this;
whether there would be some dramatic occurrence,

characterised by flashes of light and loud noises and miraculously my arm would be perfect, or whether I would simply wake up one morning and both arms would be the same. In my childish mind, I opted for the latter, and for many years as a child the first thing I would do when I woke up each morning would be to check to see if I had been touched by the healing power of Jesus during the night. My mother always talked of the celebrations we would have when this day came. She said she would buy me a beautiful new dress to wear at the party we would have. Interestingly, although I have had countless dresses since then, I still think of wearing a new dress as one of the first things I would probably do when I get healed.

Mum believed in my healing, and so I without question went along with everything she suggested or insisted on to aid this healing. My childhood, though happy and very comfortable, was punctuated by 'trips' in pursuit of healing. She did not know when or through whom this healing would come, so we never missed an opportunity, either medical or religious. I spent considerable time away from home in hospitals abroad for several months at a stretch; I missed a lot of school, and life seemed an endless cycle of going away, returning, and struggling to settle back into home and school life.

When I was five years old, after months of physiotherapy and various tests in Nigeria, we were referred to Great Ormond Street children's hospital in London. My parents were determined that there would be no delay in getting more advanced treatment for me. But at the time my sister Chioma was newly born. It took about a year for all the arrangements to be finalised with the hospital and for my mum to get the extended time off work to take me there. Agu was nine years old, Ikechi was seven, I was six, and Chioma was just one at the time. It was clear that we were going to be away for several weeks. We travelled to the UK on a British Caledonian flight from Lagos airport. It was my first trip abroad.

Now that I have children of my own, I realise the sacrifices that my parents made to ensure that I had a good future. On that first trip to England they took the unusual step, given the circumstances, of having my brothers accompany us. Chioma was left in the care of my father, our nanny who had been with us for years, and my mother's dear friend, Aunty Elsie.

We settled into Fordwych Court, an apartment complex in north-west London. I remember our great excitement as children. It just seemed like one big adventure. Almost without pause we began the hospital rounds – I really have no idea how my mother coped with carting around three young children on the numerous appointments which all seemed to be at the crack of dawn. Even with a child's perspective I knew that it was a very difficult time. But both she and my father agreed that it was absolutely essential for my future and worth any price that they had to pay. Her hopes were riding high, and she was cautiously expectant of positive news from the doctors. But after a barrage of tests the news was not what they expected. My mum was told that I was too young for the surgery that they contemplated, and that she should bring me back when I was 13 years old. Her situation was compounded early into our stay when one night Ikechi complained of a sore throat, and by the next day his face looked like he was hiding two grapefruits in both cheeks. Somehow he had managed to contract mumps at the worst possible time! It was impossible trying to keep us apart, and before long Agu's face also swelled. Mercifully I did not catch it, but I know that this period took its toll on my mother, and I still wonder how she coped.

My parents were not prepared to accept the hospital's conclusion. Returning me home seemed too much like giving up, and they thought seven years was just too long to wait. They sought another opinion, and we began another series of tests at St Mary's Hospital in Paddington. The doctors there were willing to take on my case, but the surgery anticipated was so extensive that it had to be done in three stages over a period of a year. As it was not an option for us all to remain in the UK for that length of time, Mum and Dad decided that the boys should be taken back home in time for the start of the new school year.

We flew back home. A few months later, my mum and I returned to England. This time I went into hospital and had the first of many surgeries. For this first phase, there were to be three surgeries performed at four-monthly intervals. My mother could not stay away from Nigeria for the entire period, and realised that she had to make alternative provisions for me. There was no one who could come from home to be with me, but she had a relative in London who was a nurse. She made an arrangement with her, and for the months in between each surgery I lived with Aunty Mercy and her family. She and her husband had six children, including daughters Betty and Inoino, who were roughly my age.

It was quite difficult at the beginning. They were, after all, strangers. I struggled to understand why my mum had to leave me with people I did not know. I missed my brothers and baby sister, I missed my parents, and I missed the familiarity of my own home. But they were good people, and I soon blended into the family, becoming quite inseparable from the two girls – I remember that we formed a singing group modelled after The Three Degrees, the American female vocal group that experienced great success in the 1970s. We held many after-dinner concerts for the family and friends, and Aunty Mercy even got a seamstress friend of hers to sew us identical catsuits!

Catsuits, bell bottoms and platform shoes were all the rage at the time.

I began attending school with the children whenever I was out of hospital. I had many happy memories of this time, although I was not a huge fan of hospitals and doctors. There were to be several more surgeries in the future at great cost to the family, financially and otherwise. My parents were determined to do all that they could to ensure that I had a comfortable future, and I will always be grateful for their efforts.

When my mother and I were at home in Nigeria, we went to healing crusades all over the country. We travelled long distances in search of a miracle, and as I grew older, I used to joke about people like my mother keeping healing ministries in business! Each time we returned minus expected healing, I sensed her disappointment, and as a little girl grew increasingly burdened by this. I began to wonder why I was not healed when countless others appeared to be receiving their healing so effortlessly. I questioned whether there was something in my attitude that prevented this healing from coming. Perhaps I lacked the requisite level of faith to propel my healing to reality. Perhaps there was some unresolved sin somewhere in my past for which I was being punished. Perhaps the Lord did not love me, or I did not love Him enough. I agonised over my situation.

I now realise the error in these thoughts and feelings, but at the time they were reinforced by my early experiences with 'healers'. I remember one incident in particular. During my mid-teenage years, my mother had taken me to yet another healing meeting, which she was told would be led by a lady who had the 'gift of healing'. She had been regaled with stories of people receiving their sight, hearing, mobility, speech, and being cured of all kinds of ailments. And so, we went.

My first thought when I saw the crowds at the meeting venue was, 'I am not like these people.' I was shocked to see so many with extensive disabilities and disfigurements. Everywhere I looked there were bodies in varying degrees of brokenness. The atmosphere seemed thick with despair. It was as if the people and their families looked on this lady as their last hope. I was consumed by anguish, indignation and another feeling, which I later realised was humiliation.

From where we stood, I watched as the somewhat formidable lady prayed for people's healing and then commanded them to do whatever they could not do before. Her brusque manner and the insensitivity of her helpers irritated me. In particular, I was not convinced by the healings she said had taken place and could see no visible change in the majority of people. Several people were told that their hearts were hardened and that they did not have the requisite level of faith to be healed. I remember in particular one child's heart-wrenching screams as he was held down and 'evil spirits' commanded to leave his body.

The only moment of light relief came when I had a thought for which I was certain some members of the ecclesiastic body could have condemned me. The preacher happened to be blind, and as she berated people for not having faith I remember thinking, 'Physician, heal thyself!' I did not know where these words came from but somewhere in the back of my mind I thought that it was something I had heard my mother say as I was growing up, usually in indignation. Much later I discovered, to my amusement, that they were in the Bible (Luke 4:23, KJV).

I was upset with my mother for placing me in this situation; I could tell that she was also uncomfortable about what we saw. My mood only darkened further when I was taken before the 'healer'. Her hands felt around my shoulder and neck as someone whispered in her ear what this present 'case' was.

'I am not a case,' my mind screamed in fury.

I caught snatches of conversation: 'Girl… broken arm… mother.' Her fingers rested on the back of my neck and then traced a path down towards my shoulder. They paused at the pendant that I had on. It was a gold crucifix, a gift from my mum at my Confirmation[1] a few years earlier. It meant so much to me. I derived great comfort from it, and had not taken it off since I was given it. What followed next was completely unexpected. She snatched at the crucifix, breaking the chain, and then said that it was evil to wear a graven image of the Lord. I had no idea what a graven image was, but in my mind I interpreted her words to mean that I was doing something evil. One of the assistants was given the broken chain and crucifix, and she handed them to me without so much as an apology.

Hot tears filled my eyes and made everything in my line of vision dance around for a moment before spilling onto my T-shirt. I yanked my hand across my eyes, furious with myself for showing signs of weakness, furious with my mother for putting me in that position, furious with life for having dealt me those cards. With steely resolve I vowed that I would never again allow myself to be placed in this situation. I was done with 'healers'. Being 'done' with healers meant that I avoided them completely.

From the outset, my mother struggled to accept my decision. Although we always came away from these crusades without the much sought-after healing, she was undeterred and simply looked for the next, more 'powerful' conduit through which this healing would become reality. There was no shortage of likely candidates. Someone always happened to know somebody who recommended a powerful man or woman with 'the gift'. Each time she came to me with suggestions about 'seeing someone' my response was swift, but she was determined for a long time and would always broach the subject tentatively.

'Darling, there is someone I'd like you to meet,' she'd say innocently.

'Who?' my eyes became slits as I peered at her, unable to hide the mix of suspicion and frustration. 'Here we go again,' I would think. The humiliation from my previous encounters with healers still stung.

'This woman…' And then would follow a brief summation of what she had done and what qualified her to be a potential channel of God's healing power in my situation.

As Mum spoke I would sigh deeply, waiting for her to finish.

'I'm not going,' I would say quietly.

Mum would plough on determined, her mind focused on one thing only.

'Mummy, I am not going,' I would repeat.

One day I turned to her and said carefully, 'Mummy, why won't you let it rest? I'm all right the way I am. If God chooses to heal my arm then I don't think He needs any help, and in the meantime I want to get on with living the best way I know how.'

This was the first time that I had expressed my feelings so clearly. In actual fact, it was the most I had ever said on the subject. It was hard, very hard. I could see hurt in her eyes. I did not want to hurt my mother: she was wonderful; we were close and shared many intimacies, but I knew that this unrelenting search for healing was beginning to drive a wedge between us.

'Why can't she just be happy with my life as it is?' I was perplexed and a little frustrated. But a part of me recognised that as far as she was concerned, to do so would be to give up, and my mother was not the giving-up type. She loved me too much.

It was a complex situation, and I realised that she felt, perhaps even more deeply than I did, the pain of my disability. I knew that she worried about my future, although she never said anything to me. I, on the other hand, had a peace about my future; I never thought that I would be disadvantaged in any way. I just knew that it would be a good future, despite my challenges. I don't know where the confidence came from; it was just there.

Neither my siblings nor Dad knew of Mother's search for my divine healing. My father was not given to religious expression, and his attendance at church was limited to weddings, christenings, and funerals. When I dug my heels in and refused to budge my mum had nowhere to turn. She knew that she would get no support from him on the subject, and so she ultimately let it rest.

My way of protecting my emotions was to deny that I had a disability. I thought that if I coped with life so well, then I would never have to acknowledge that I needed healing, and would therefore not have to face the disappointment of not being healed at healing meetings and crusades. Thus began an elaborate cover-up that lasted years and almost became an obsession. I was propelled by an irrational urge to do things better than everyone else. I pushed myself relentlessly and adopted standards that were unrealistic and unhealthy. All public displays of weakness were banished, and I would never ask for help nor accept it when offered.

As my relationship with Jesus has deepened, I have begun the process of self-examination; stripping away the façade that had cocooned me for so long. I have learned to be honest about my needs and desires. I recently began a study of Jesus' healing ministry. I discovered that Jesus was always sensitive and careful to protect the dignity of the people He healed. He never accused or humiliated them, and He had ultimate confidence in His healing powers and His authority. Yet it is necessary to emphasise the place of importance that belief plays in healing. Belief is always present when the miracle-working power of God is exercised on behalf of a person, and Jesus always commended faith wherever He encountered it (see Mark 10:52, 'Go your way; your faith has made you well', NKJV), but it is not always the belief of the recipient that is the determining factor; for instance, the paralysed man was healed because Jesus saw the faith of his friends (Mark 2:1–5, NKJV).

God's power at work in us

The Bible makes many references to Jesus' compassion towards people. He is able to 'understand and sympathize ... with our weaknesses and infirmities'.[2] He healed a pre-teen with a kind word, 'Little girl, get up!' he said gently,[3] and helped a feverish older woman to sit up;[4] to a woman who struggled with a debilitating condition and insecurity issues and who had been treated as an outcast, he said, 'Daughter, your faith has made you well.'[5] He did not berate a desperate father who honestly acknowledged his feelings of doubt, but restored his tormented son to mental wholeness and stability.[6] Jesus was kindness personified. He did not castigate people in their weakness. More importantly, He emphasised the point that a disability is not the result of someone having sinned. In the story of the blind man in Luke's Gospel, Jesus was quick to reject the assumption that his condition was punishment for a sinful act by either him or his parents.

> Jesus answered, It was not that this man or his parents sinned, but he was born blind in order that the workings of God should be manifested (displayed and illustrated) in him.
> (John 9:3)

This being the case, then people who have been entrusted with the healing power of the Lord must execute that awesome responsibility with the same compassionate nature that Jesus always demonstrated. Just as He had done, they should be mindful to protect the dignity of the person to whom they are ministering.

For many years after this experience, I was adamant in my refusal to attend healing services. If a service was tagged as a healing service I avoided it like the plague. But despite my best efforts, I sometimes found myself in services where people were healed, even though they never started out as healing services. On those occasions, I would refuse the preacher's invitation to stand up or come forward if healing was needed. When I did stand up, I did so under duress. I hated any attention being drawn to me, and I was so certain that there had to be another way which did not involve all that angst. It always seemed as though there was a reason why I was not getting healed when other people were. We were constantly being told that God wanted to heal everyone; that Jesus had made healing available for us all through His death on the cross.

I remember saying to the Lord, 'You can just as easily heal me in the privacy of my bedroom!'

I often wonder how many people like me have been put off healing ministries because of bad experiences.

Thankfully, my experiences never shook my faith; they just made me more determined to get on with life as best I could. At some point I reached what I considered to be a comfortable place for me. I decided that everyone had a cross to bear, and perhaps this was my own cross. Interestingly, I never doubted the fact that Jesus could heal; what I was not so sure about was whether He would heal me, Chizor. It was easier for me to accept that perhaps healing was something that only happened to other people, rather than endure the torment of trying to figure out why it was not happening to me.

Since then I have come to know Jesus a lot better, in particular, Jesus the Healer. I know now and truly believe that it is God's will to heal; sickness and infirmity are not His plan for us. I will never stop looking to Him for healing, and I will never stop applying His Word to my circumstances. For all that we had been through together and all that we had shared, I had hoped that my healing would happen in my mother's lifetime. I wanted so much for her to witness that day. Even more than I wanted my healing for myself, I wanted it for her. In my mind, it would have been compensation for her pain and suffering; having children of my own has given me a better understanding of the challenges she must have faced. When she passed away in 2009, one of my initial sorrows was the fact that she did not see this healing. But I think that there was an even bigger issue at play – my mum had the opportunity to see Jesus working in and through me, in spite of my challenges. I believe that my life spoke a more powerful message than my healing all those years ago could ever have done.

I realise that I have come a long way. On this journey I was able to acknowledge, without guilt and without feeling selfish, that I wanted to be healed; I knew that it would make an inexpressible difference to my life. Then in time I got to the stage where I was openly expectant about being healed. I looked forward with unconcealed eagerness to that moment. Some days I would wonder what I would do once I had been healed. When they were younger, I thought that I would put plaits in my daughters' hair, but now they are grown up and this is no longer a need. I did have one abiding thought; I have always wanted to use a skipping rope unaided and, in addition, I thought that perhaps I would buy that long-awaited dress after all!

Yet more time elapsed, the journey continued and through life's experiences I have noticed that an interesting thing has happened to me, but I cannot say when exactly it did. Increasingly, my healing is no longer a focus for me. Whilst I still hope for and expect it, I can truly say that it matters less than it did before. I am able to look beyond it, and I can now embrace more wholeheartedly the rest of my life without my arm being healed. Today I can truthfully say that if Jesus never heals me in the manner that I had hoped for all those years ago, if He has a greater plan for me as I am, then I am more than all right with it. My life is full and rich. I have been blessed in countless ways and I am grateful, very grateful.

---

[1] Confirmation is a rite which is carried out in some Christian traditions (e.g. Anglican) by the laying on of hands by a confirming bishop. Viewed as a sacrament, it is the point at which someone who has been christened as a baby affirms for themselves the faith they have been baptised into, and their intention to live a life of commitment to Christ. See https://www.churchofengland.org/our-faith/confirmation/what-is-confirmation.aspx (accessed 27th May 2015).

[2] Hebrews 4:15.

[3] Mark 5:41, NLT.

[4] Mark 1:29–31.

[5] Mark 5:34, NLT.

[6] Mark 9:17–27.

Chapter eight
God the matchmaker: marriage and disability

> What greater thing is there for two human souls than to feel
> that they are joined for life – to strengthen each other in all
> labour, to rest on each other in all sorrow, to minister to each
> other in all pain, to be one with each other in silent,
> unspeakable memories at the moment of the last parting?
> (George Eliot, 1819–80[1])

From very early on, I thought a lot about marriage. It seemed to me to be a natural progression for any young girl and was the expectation of the society in which I was raised. Although I did not do much dating in my adolescent years, I had this unshakeable belief that I would get married. I had two younger sisters with several years between us, and very early on I assumed the self-imposed responsibility of looking after them. I thought it would be great fun to have little people of my own, and looked towards marriage with eager anticipation.

I always said that I thought I was ready to be married from around the age of 18; what stood in my way was just the small matter of the husband presenting himself! My assurance was such that I announced to my mother on one of my trips home for Christmas that this would be the last Christmas I would spend in our family home as a single girl. The conversation went something like this:

'The next time I come home it will be for my wedding.'

'What do you mean?' she asked, looking up from her newspaper.

'This will be my last Christmas in this house as a single girl,' I repeated calmly.

Eyes narrowing, she sat up straight in her chair. 'Have you met someone?'

I could tell that she was perplexed. I smiled, full of mischief. I knew she was wondering whether this was another one of my 'secrets'.

'No, but I'll be married within the next year!'

My mother had the most expressive eyes which spoke a language of their own. One look from those eyes could strike terror in the hearts of grown men, and keep boisterous children in check; those eyes had corralled my siblings and me when we were little. At that moment they registered confusion and uncertainty. What exactly was I saying?

I smiled mysteriously. My siblings and I loved to tease our mother. We took great delight in winding her up, and at that moment I could tell that she was indeed all wound up.

Interestingly, when I said this, no one had expressed any kind of interest in walking me down the aisle. Although I had known Bajo for a few years, we were little more than casual friends at the time. In actual fact, I did not think much of him, and there was definitely no romantic tug between us. All of this changed in a relatively short period. Within a few months, he appeared to have taken an interest in me. To my amusement he began to grow on me gradually and without fanfare. Soon we were planning our wedding. I am still intrigued by the calmness with which I approached marriage. I think that it was definitely God's grace; we were meant to be together – I have never been more certain of anything. My next trip back home to Nigeria after I spoke those memorable words to my mum was to get married!

I remember that my mum was stunned when I told her about Bajo.

'You haven't given me enough time to plan things properly,' she exclaimed, a little perturbed.

'But I told you last Christmas that my next trip home would be to get married,' was my casual reply.

She gave me 'the look', started to answer but decided that it was probably better to channel her energy towards the huge preparations that a wedding for her first daughter would require.

Walking in God's plan

I had numerous thoughts on marriage. I wanted a strong marriage, a home filled with love and the sound of giggling children. Bajo and I were thrilled to discover that we both wanted the same things. I was excited about the future, our future. I looked forward to us growing and 'becoming'. I looked forward to getting to know him as the days and years went by until we became, as I often described, like 'old socks'! Old socks are familiar and comfortable; they fit your feet perfectly, provide warmth and security, and you never want to discard them. But I never bargained on the fact that I would permanently be under the direct scrutiny of someone else. For me, marriage was my first experience of complete openness with another human being.

My husband asked the questions that no one had ever asked before, and he insisted on replies. He challenged me to confront feelings and hurts that had been concealed for so long. In marriage you are accountable to someone else – someone who is determined to pursue your progressive development. A major challenge for me a short period into our marriage was the realisation that I could no longer hide. I was compelled to begin the process of renewing my mind. As I have walked through uncharted territory, I have had the support and encouragement of my husband. With him, I feel safe enough to reveal my innermost thoughts and fears. Together we mapped out a strategy for my personal development and goals to chart my progress.

Despite my initial trepidation, I approached marriage with a strong sense that I was walking in God's plan for my life. I felt that Bajo had been prepared especially for me, and vice versa. When Bajo eventually asked me to marry him, I said I would think about it. I had heard somewhere that a woman should not be too eager to accept a marriage proposal! I laugh now when I think about my behaviour. And so I 'thought' about his proposal, and he waited for my response, praying more than he ever had in his life up to that point.

Give me Your eyes, Lord

One cold winter day, I took a long walk from my parents' flat in north-west London, which I shared with my sisters, to our brother's home – a distance of about three miles. I needed to make a decision, and I wanted to be sure that it was the right one. I hoped that the crisp air would blow away the cobwebs that seemed to be clogging up my head, so that I could think clearly. I had not planned on walking the entire journey and kept walking whilst I talked to the Lord.

'Give me Your eyes, dear Lord; let me see what You see when You look at Bajo,' I muttered.

The moment those words left my lips, I thought, 'What an odd thing to ask for.'

It may have been an unusual request, but I knew that I really could not trust my own eyes, for they were likely to see things which might in the long run be trivial and shallow. I wanted to see beyond what my own eyes revealed, and only God, who knows the end from the beginning, could help me. I arrived at my brother's home and talked at length with my late sister-in-law, Ify, with whom I had shared many significant experiences since she became a part of our family. She had a quiet wisdom that belied her years, and talking with her was like having mist lift from before my eyes. Suddenly I could see much more clearly, and I truly believed that God had answered my prayers and had given me His eyes! I saw things about Bajo that I had not seen previously, and I felt safe and certain in the knowledge that I was making the right decision.

When I eventually said 'yes' to him, he displayed a level of joy that I have seen in him at certain times in our marriage. It is difficult to capture his excitement with words. We set about the task of planning our wedding with unshakeable certainty. We had no doubt that we were God's choice for one another.

On our wedding day, I could almost picture Him looking down at us, the Benevolent Father watching as we took our vows. The importance of every word that we spoke at the ceremony resonated deep within me. Bajo and I made a covenant with each other, but more importantly, we made a covenant with God. He was the central, most important Person in our union. I glanced across at my father as he steeled himself for the tough task of giving his first daughter away in marriage. To this day I struggle to put into words the look on his face. He had done such a wonderful job of protecting me from the harsh realities of life, and I know that he was concerned about whom

I would marry. I remember that he soon pronounced Bajo, my husband, to be all right; a gentle, kind person, and the sort of man with whom he could entrust his child.

'For richer, for poorer, in sickness and in health,' I said, my voice stronger than I expected.

''Til death us do part.' He grinned his trademark toothy grin.

'Amen.'

So be it.

We smiled.

I knew that whatever the obstacles we encountered in the future, we would be all right with God on our side to guide and shield us.

Nonetheless, there were obstacles to encounter and overcome. When Bajo decided to marry me, he knew that there would be questions; perhaps some resistance, even. A relative asked him how we would cope with life. His amused response was, 'Wait until you meet her!'

My 'disability' has never been something that I have allowed to define me.

No hiding place

Marriage demands honesty and openness. I struggled initially with the thought of complete vulnerability. It is very difficult to expose something that you have spent a lifetime hiding. For several years I had covered up my body, avoiding mirrors that showed my full length, wearing clothes that took the focus away from my arm. I had got to the stage where I believed that I had attained a degree of success in this elaborate cover-up. Marriage demolished my carefully constructed walls.

I remember that Bajo would hold my arm, gently, refusing to allow me to wriggle out of his grasp. It was horribly uncomfortable, but he was determined. He would watch me, constantly (and still does), a huge smile stamped on his face.

'Stop watching me!' I would snap.

'Why?' was his speedy retort. 'I like what I see!'

I lost count of the number of times he said, 'It is OK. I love you, all of you. I want you to be comfortable with me. Please don't hide yourself from me.'

It has taken me years not just simply to hear, but to begin to believe and accept that there is truth in his words. Today I am completely at ease with him; he reads me and anticipates my needs. Being at ease with him means that he is my extra hand whenever I need it. He does up fiddly buttons, adjusts clothing, does up the clasps on jewellery; he is my sous chef and, on very rare occasions, has even proven himself as a hairdresser!

In the past, whenever I ate out, and especially if I was with unfamiliar company, rather than ask for help I would order items from the menu that did not require much effort to cut up. I lost count of the times that I would select a meal option that was a second or third choice. This is no longer the case. Now, when we eat out, as soon as my meal is delivered to the table, Bajo will watch first to see if I can tackle the food with just a fork. If after an attempt it turns out to be too tough, I simply rest my fork on the plate and this is his signal to slide my plate over; then he sets to work cutting up a steak or a lamb chop. He knows how particular I am, and so he is very careful not to mess up the plate; he also knows not to cut the food up so small that it looks like a toddler's meal. He will then slide it back to me without a word. An observer would probably be fascinated by this exchange because no words pass between us. Interestingly, we never agreed what to do, we just happened to fall into this pattern after an initial challenging period.

When we first got married, it annoyed me that Bajo wanted to do everything for me. I would bristle each time that he tried. He felt his role as husband demanded that he 'took care of me'. Whilst we both agreed with this in principle (and what woman would not!), we disagreed on just what this meant. He felt he had to do everything for me, and I was coming from a place where my independence was very important to me. We locked horns for a time until I learned that accepting help did not make me helpless. He learned that, for me, being independent had a wider implication in that it meant exercising choice, control, and freedom. We eventually reached a compromise which involves me accepting help, and him watching first rather than just wading in to take over. One day, a few years in, it was clear how far I had come when I let him do things that I was more than capable of handling on my own.

Now, after 18 years of marriage we function like clockwork. Social gatherings, particularly buffets and cocktail-style dos, which are standing only, had always proved a little tricky for me; it is impossible to hold a drink and a plate in one hand. I tried to avoid them as much as possible, but for many years they were part of my working environment, and there have been times when I would eat nothing, simply because I could not hold a plate with a glass and did not want to draw any attention to myself. Whenever we go together to such gatherings, Bajo will get my plate and then hold on to it whilst I eat. He does it so easily and without fuss. He is always watching over me, always mindful and solicitous. We might be in a roomful of people and separated by some distance; he might be engaged in conversations with other people, but he is always attentive. There is a certain assurance that his presence brings. Whereas in the past I would feel self-conscious, this is no longer the case. Our life may not follow a conventional path, but it is our life and our marriage. We have found what works for us. I realise all too well that only God, who knew us even before we were born, could have orchestrated the course of our lives in the manner that He has; only He could have prepared us so perfectly for one another.

I am grateful for having Bajo by my side, constantly supporting and always reassuring. But much more than his presence is the awareness that God Himself is there.

---

[1] George Eliot, *Adam Bede* (Wordsworth Classics, Wordsworth Editions Limited 1997). Used with permission.

Chapter nine
Motherhood

It has been said that life has treated me harshly; and
sometimes I have complained in my heart because many
pleasures of human experience have been withheld from me,
but when I recollect the treasure of friendship that has been
bestowed upon me I withdraw all charges against life. If much
has been denied me, much, very much has been given me.
So long as the memory of certain beloved friends lives in my
heart I shall say that life is good.
(Helen Keller, American Educator, Journalist and
Humanitarian, 1880–1968[1])

My greatest challenge was having and caring for our baby. I was
apprehensive, but undeterred. I have always loved babies, and I
always knew that I would have my own. There was just
something about babies that tugged at my heartstrings. I had had
a little practice with my nephew and niece, who were the first
grandchildren in my family. I had been very much a part of their
mother's pregnancies and was there when they were born. My
nephew was the first baby in the family, and his mother and I
shared his care in the first five months of his life. So I felt that I
was ready. I thought that motherhood was written next to my
name!

Bajo and I had our first child, a sweet little girl, exactly one year into our marriage. Her arrival was full of drama, turbulence, and unspeakable joy. After a relatively uneventful eight months, things began to deteriorate rapidly in the last few weeks of my pregnancy, for no reason that was medically apparent initially. But in a matter of a few days, I developed a severe case of pre-eclampsia which led to an early delivery by emergency Caesarean section. She was little, the smallest baby I had seen thus far at just over four pounds in weight. I stared at this tiny person who was completely dependent on me. Everything I thought I knew disappeared in that moment. I panicked. How would I look after her? What sort of mother would I be? As if reading my mind, Bajo said, 'She's blessed to have you as her mother. Everything will be all right.'

There is always a way

That first night in the hospital, after Bajo had gone home for a few hours rest, I was awakened by our baby's cries. The sound seemed to pierce the darkness in the room. Still sore from the surgery, I found that I could barely move. Even the slightest movement sent stabbing pains shooting through my body. I lay helplessly watching her, hoping she would settle down again. Her cries increased, and I knew instinctively that she needed to be close to me.

'Someone will come soon,' I thought, trying to reassure myself. I held my breath. No one came. Baby howled. Frustrated by the non-appearance of the nursing staff, I knew that I had to do something. Gritting my teeth I began a crab-like shuffle to the edge of my bed, dragging the intravenous tube with me. She howled even louder. I leaned across and tried to pick her up but found that I could barely reach her, let alone lift her with one very encumbered hand. I lay there wondering what to do, hoping that someone would come soon. I squeezed my eyes shut, thinking hard.

Seconds ticked by like hours. Still, no one appeared. The baby howled all the louder. I tried desperately to quell the feeling of panic that was racing through me like a runaway train. Then, as I had done countless times in the past when faced with a challenging situation, I whispered, 'Please help me, dear Lord.' It was as though He had been waiting for me. Suddenly a picture flashed across my mind. I remembered the cartoons I had watched as a child when a stork would bring babies to their mothers – the babies would be wrapped up in a bit of cloth, held within the stork's beak as it flew to deliver 'baby duck' to Mr and Mrs Duck of Ducktown! I smiled in the dark when I realised what this picture meant. Leaning as far as I could, I gathered up my baby in her blanket, scooping her up in the bedclothes with my good arm, just as I had seen in the cartoons. Transporting her slowly across the expanse of space, I prayed that she would not fall out of this hastily made sling. Thankfully she reached my bed without incident. I wrapped her in my arms, holding her close, and she soon quietened down. As I rocked her gently, a little voice in my heart whispered, 'There is always a way.'

God takes care of the details

I spent the rest of the night just watching my daughter, whom we had named 'Risachi' (a name that has its origins in the Ibo language and means 'remember God'). I felt the Lord say to me, 'I gave you this child. You can look after her; I have taken care of the details.' I was to know the significance of these words in the coming days and months.

Although my baby was small, she was the right size for me, and I could balance her on my right arm and manage her weight (which was just over that of a two kilogramme bag of sugar) without difficulty. Although I was a relative novice, she seemed to know just what to do; she stared at me for long periods through big, dark eyes as I talked to her for hours on end. I referred to these times as our 'getting to know you' moments. We were in the hospital for several days following complications related to her birth, and though it did not seem so at the time, that was a blessing in disguise. Whilst my body healed, I was learning to care for my child in the safety of the hospital environment, where I knew that help was only a few feet away. I was soon to realise what God's 'taking care of the details' meant.

As I said, Risachi was very small, and light as the proverbial feather. When I got over my initial terror, I found that she fitted neatly in the crook of my right arm, leaving my good arm free to feed her. Had she been a much heavier child, I would have struggled to support her weight, particularly as she grew. The Lord had given me the perfectly sized baby, slightly bigger than a child's doll.

My confidence grew with each passing day. I learned to change nappies with one hand, and became quite adept at bathing, dressing, feeding, burping. Whilst I was learning, Risachi would simply gaze up at me. She was a very even-tempered baby. On one of those early nights after a feed, I watched the sky change colour from the inky blackness of the night to the pink-tinged orange of a perfect winter's morning, without flourish, without incident. I thought, this child is as placid as the arrival of the dawn. She had the sort of eyes that seemed to communicate things she could not possibly know of. Nothing seemed to faze her, as I pulled and tugged at clothing, muttering over and over, 'Sorry, baby... sorry, my precious child,' worried that the vests stayed too long over her face, trying to make sure that her tiny fingers did not get caught in the sleepsuits, and trying to support her head with one arm. She just stared, accommodating my jerky actions. Her silence was so reassuring during those fledgling days of motherhood.

We were eventually let out of hospital into the waiting arms of my mother, who had left her hectic schedule to come and support me. As always, my family formed a protective shield around me. After a fortnight confined to the restrictive hospital environment, I was ready to take the next step, to embrace life with my girl. When I was a child, I played a game which I called 'one step at a time'. If there was anything looming ahead that made me a little anxious, I would break the time into manageable tasks which I would tick off one at a time. The next step for me as a new mum was being entirely on my own with Risachi. I felt that this would be my real test.

Finally, the time came for mother to return home and for Bajo to return to work. We had prepared as best as we could for that day. Bajo had cooked lots of easy meals and stocked up the freezer. He had given me lots of pep talks, and I had stocked up on confidence. I imagined what I would do when we were entirely on our own, and kept whispering to myself, 'One step at a time, Chizor.'

He was concerned because we lived in a village just outside Brighton, East Sussex, about two hours away from our family, and he was working in central London, almost two and a half hours away. Much too soon the day arrived. Bajo was due to catch the 6.40 a.m. train and left the house at 6 a.m. Before he left, he made me a light breakfast, lunch and snacks which only needed to be microwaved, then he set everything I might need within easy reach. Risachi had been given her early feed and put back to sleep; if she followed the usual pattern then she should stay asleep for the next two to three hours.

But that first day we were alone, any pattern that I thought Risachi had went out the door with her father. A few minutes after he left, her eyes flew open, and they stayed open for the best part of the day. She squalled each time I tried to place her in her Moses basket. I ended up holding her the entire day, attempting to grab a bite with her in my arms, and even having to use the bathroom still holding her. When Bajo returned that night, I was so exhausted I handed her to him at the door without a word, turned around and went to bed. We survived our first day alone and very many days after.

One issue constantly weighed on my mind – the question of what to do with my daughter's hair. I wondered how I would put plaits in her hair as my mother had done mine; I often thought that it would have been easier to care for a little boy, who would need nothing more than the occasional haircut. Then I reminded myself that the course of my life had sometimes gone down challenging routes, but I had always found help along the way. I knew having children would be no different, and so I simply looked at it as one more hurdle in this journey of life that I needed to overcome.

Each day, I combed Risachi's hair and dressed her with care, awaiting with nervous anticipation the day when her hair would be long enough to braid. As I waited, I gathered a stockpile of hair ruffles in every conceivable colour. When that day came, I spent hours one morning attempting to make my fingers work and do what I had done countless times in my head. I was frustrated but refused to give up. All the while my baby slept the blissful sleep of ignorance – she was three months old. I finally realised that I could use the toes of my right foot just like fingers and within a very slow hour I had her hair in cute little balls with colourful hair bubbles. She looked beautiful, and I had an indescribable sense of accomplishment. When Bajo came home, his excitement could not be contained as he whooped with joy. This was our moment of victory – one more battle had been fought and won.

As time passed, I became adept at doing Risachi's hair, and often had it done in less than 15 minutes. When she grew older, was more mobile and less inclined to sit still, we decided that Bajo would be my other hand and I taught him what to do. We were raising our children together, and early on we had decided that each task concerning their care could be taught or learned. Many times when the girls were little, they would announce with great pride to anyone who cared to listen that 'Daddy made their hair'!

Bajo and I are a team; when I need an extra hand, he is that. When I insist on 'doing it myself', he steps back and allows me to find my way. No one but God could have made such a provision for our future by placing us together.

As they grew older, I saw several examples of God taking care of the details. Whilst Bajo was wonderful as a budding hairdresser, I wanted my girls' hair to always look neat and well-made, and his skills were still in the rookie stages. I had very few options, and this bothered me greatly. We lived in a village far away from any hairdressers that specialised in Afro-Caribbean hair, and our visits to London where there was no shortage of hairdressers were infrequent.

One day, a young lady moved to Brighton and started attending our church. We met her, and before long it became apparent that she was another one of those special people whose path God allows to cross yours for a whole host of reasons. She has since become family to us. Aunty Tally, as the girls call her, was many things, including a whizz at styling hair. She had a gentleness about her, and a love for our girls which was definitely God-inspired. She did their hair each week for five years, until we moved away from Sussex. Even then, God had gone ahead of me. Another lady walked up to me at church one day and said she felt the Lord was asking her to take over doing my girls' hair for the foreseeable future. I was not at all surprised, just deeply moved by God's faithfulness. She did their hair for four years!

Seeing God in every challenge

Our second child arrived in even more challenging circumstances than her older sister. With our history, the doctors were more prepared for the 'unexpected' and were taking no chances. Unhappy with the results of a routine check one morning, I was sent immediately by my doctor to our local emergency room. There followed a barrage of tests, and then I was given the unwelcome news that I would not be going home any time soon.

It seemed too much like déjà vu. I remained in hospital for several weeks. Without warning, Bajo had to mind the home and take care of Risachi, who was just over two years old. Days turned into weeks, and I began to feel as though I had been forgotten in a hospital ward that sometimes had only me as a patient. During the weekdays, I had lots of time on my hands, as visitors came mostly at the weekend; Bajo could only visit during his lunch break, and in the evenings, when he brought Risachi. And so I read non-stop, and I spent many hours talking to God. I asked many questions and kept a journal of what I felt were His answers. It was not an easy time. But I could not deny that God was with me. I worried about many things, especially about Risachi, who could not understand why 'baby and Mama were not going home' with her and Dada. There were always tears at the end of each visit, and it just broke my heart.

I had begun to rely on Bajo for so much, and I would feel a little anxious whenever he had to go home. One night I could not sleep at all. The nights were the most challenging; the hours stretched out so long. Each time the doctors came by on their ward rounds, their prognosis seemed bleaker. We were faced with the real possibility that the baby would be born early, and we were just trying to buy time. Every day was crucial, and more time gave her a better chance for survival. It was a fine balancing act between the need to keep the baby in me for longer, and the risk that the continued pregnancy had to mine and her health.

Very early on the morning of the 1st August 2000, three and a half weeks after I had first set foot in the hospital, the decision was made to deliver the baby by emergency Caesarean section. The night before, Bajo had dropped off Risachi at my brother's home as he was due to attend a job interview that morning – I had heard somewhere that some of the most stressful things that a person goes through in their lifetime included marriage, the birth of a baby, a new job, or new home. We were attempting three out of that list simultaneously. According to our planning, the baby was not due for another ten weeks, and we were due to move into a bigger house during the first week in August. Bajo was looking for a better job in view of the needs of our growing family.

I thought I had worked out things very carefully, but sometimes life does not unfold according to plan. Here I was, trapped in hospital; moving day could not be altered, and the baby seemed determined to arrive on the day her father was away on a job interview. When the decision to deliver her was made, the hospital tried to reach Bajo without success; at the time, he was on a train with no reception. Every member of my family was at least two hours away. I had no one that I knew with me, but the Lord told me clearly that I would not be alone and that He had made provision for all the help that I would need.

The first in a line of helpers was a lovely nurse who asked whether I would mind her praying for me. This in itself was unusual, and was the beginning of a series of events that told me that God had His eye on me. The next was a wonderful anaesthetist who seemed to have eyes that I imagined Jesus' eyes would look like. They were the only part of his face that I could see in the slit between his paper hat and surgical mask. He was calm and unruffled. I could hear the smile in his voice.

Two years earlier I had had a horrible experience with the anaesthesia when Risachi was born, and I was terrified that there could be a recurrence. He promised that it would not happen again, and somehow I believed him. He talked to me about cricket; England had been playing at the Lord's Cricket Ground, and he was a fan. I did not care for cricket; the closest I had come to the game was watching our first XI cricket team play when I was at school, which was compulsory for all pupils. I wondered how he could talk of something so inconsequential at such a fraught time, but the more I listened the more I relaxed. Soon I had forgotten about my first nasty experience, and true to his word it all went smoothly. Cricket Man promised that he would not leave my side, and that he would tell me exactly what was going on behind the blue surgical curtain that separated us from the surgeon and the rest of the medical team. In less than five minutes, he announced Rinnah's birth. I cannot recall hearing her cry, but Cricket Man assured me that she was all right. I got to see her for a brief moment before she was whisked away to the Special Care Baby Unit. Soon afterwards, I was wheeled into the recovery room. Cricket Man had not once left my side. A nurse came to tell me that my sister wanted to see me, and it was only then that Cricket Man left, after wishing me well for the future.

My 'sister' was a wonderful girl whom I had met shortly after we got married and moved to Brighton. Dele was another addition to my growing list of Godsends, becoming like one of my biological sisters, and had all but adopted Risachi as her own. Bajo had called her to let her know that the baby was to be delivered that morning, and she had come right away. She stayed with me the entire day until Bajo and the rest of my family arrived. God had been so faithful; as I had asked of Him, He had ensured that I was not alone for one moment during what was a very difficult time.

A day later, I was wheeled up two floors to meet our little girl. She had arrived nine weeks premature, very ill, but with an indomitable will to live. I watched her quietly, my eyes slowly absorbing the picture before me. She was hooked up to all sorts of tubes and gadgets, separated from me by the impersonal plastic of the incubator. It was very difficult not to be moved by what I saw and heard; the flashing lights and ominous beeps did nothing to settle my mind. I breathed in deeply and expelled my breath in one long sigh. It seemed that each challenge we encountered surpassed the previous one. I wondered what the future held for us all.

In that moment, the Lord reminded me that my life would bring glory to His name, and that my weaknesses and adversities would be the backdrop for His strength. He reminded me of the name that He had given us for this child, His child. Almost two years earlier, early one morning, I was reading the Bible when I came across what I considered to be one of the most beautiful names. I had a strong impression that this would be the name of our second child, who would be a girl. Risachi was only a few months old at the time. And so we called the baby 'Rinnah', a

Hebrew name which means 'joy' and a 'shout of rejoicing in triumph'. I recalled God's faithfulness at the time of Risachi's birth and I knew that with His help, no future challenge would be insurmountable. As with her sister before her, we knew what she would be called long before she was conceived. It was interesting how those names fitted perfectly the circumstances of their births.

Rinnah was tiny, even smaller than her sister was, at a little over one kilogramme. In the days leading up to her birth, I had been given an injection in the thigh which was to speed up the development of her lungs in order to give her the best possible chance. Unsurprisingly, when she did arrive at just 30 weeks and three days, she needed the help of the professionals in the Special Care Baby Unit. We were told that she was likely to be there for at least nine weeks, up until the time when she would have been born. But Rinnah's recovery was accelerated at a speed that took the doctors by surprise.

About four weeks after her birth, I arrived at the hospital one day to be greeted with the news that they would let her out the following day, after I had spent a night in the hospital with her to prepare me for the task of taking care of her. We were elated. My hopes of resuming a normal life as a family appeared to be within our grasp. It had been a difficult couple of months, and I had found it particularly challenging to return home without our baby. Risachi could not comprehend why the baby was not at home with us, and was becoming quite clingy whenever I had to leave the house.

The night was long but uneventful. Morning finally came, and our young family was reunited as we went home to begin another season. As with all the storms that we have encountered, the Lord led us through to higher ground.

At the time that I completed the first draft of this book, Rinnah was an active four-year-old with a unique sense of humour and an infectious laugh. Her laughter had the effect of making a grey day suddenly seem brighter. It is sometimes difficult to reconcile her turbulent entry into life with the present. Today she is a bubbly, highly sociable 14-year-old, going on 30! She still carries about her the unique ability to light up a room. Bajo and I marvel when we look at her. She makes an amazing team with her sister, and I am greatly humbled just knowing that they were given to us. In my family, I have been blessed richly and beyond measure. Our Father, who is no 'respecter of persons' (Acts 10:34, KJV), does not play favourites, and is willing to do the same for you.

---

[1] Helen Keller, *Midstream – My Later Life* (New York: Doubleday, 1929), p. 67.

Chapter ten
A work in progress

God loves you just the way you are, but He loves you too
much to leave you the way you are.
(John Mason)[1]

I think of Christianity as a lifelong exercise in character
development. Life is all about growth and change. It is not a
hurried process, and I've come to realise that very seldom do you
get to skip stages. Moses' story and the various stages in his
development have long intrigued me, and I am encouraged just
reading about his experiences. When Moses is given the
assignment of demanding the Israelites' release from Egypt, we
see him outlining to the Lord in great detail the reasons why he
is completely unsuitable.

> Then Moses said to the LORD, 'O my Lord, I *am* not eloquent,
> neither before nor since You have spoken to Your servant; but
> I *am* slow of speech and slow of tongue.'
> (Exodus 4:10, NKJV)

What he was saying in effect is this: 'Lord, I am not the man
for the job; you need to choose someone who is better suited for
the task. I am not qualified. I cannot speak, I get tongue-tied and

cannot get my words out. How could I possibly speak on Your behalf?'

God's response is very interesting.

So the LORD said to him, 'Who has made man's mouth? Or who makes the mute, the deaf, the seeing, or the blind? *Have not I, the Lord?* Now therefore, go, and I will be with your mouth and teach you what you shall say.'
(Exodus 4:11–12, NKJV)

In summary, God said, 'I am God, I made you. I can unravel any twists in your speech. Just keep going, and at the right time I will teach you what to say.'

Interestingly, this Moses of stuttering lips is described in the book of Acts as one who was skilful in words and speech. Something miraculous had happened to him. Although he started out insecure and fearful, he was a work in progress. It is worth noting that by the time he is given the Ten Commandments, he is able to speak with great confidence and no longer has need of the services of his brother, Aaron. He finally becomes what he was destined to be, one who was 'mighty (powerful) in his speech and deeds' (Acts 7:22).

When God looked at him he saw a powerful orator at a time when Moses stammered. Similarly, when God looks at each of us He sees the gifts and talents that He placed in us long before we were born. I firmly believe that God, the Giver of all life, has a plan and purpose for every life, regardless of the nature or extent of one's disability. Whereas the world views people as they are at present, God looks at us as He made us to be. It is with this end, this purpose, in sight that He relates to us. If you allow God to begin to work on and in you, He will lead you through the transitional phase during which He brings out all the qualities that were put in you at birth. You will then become the person He intended you to be, wholly capable of fulfilling your purpose and destiny.

Dr Myles Monroe, author of several works on releasing and maximising potential, wrote these words:

> Too many people are mere products of their environment, allowing themselves to be victimized by the opinions of others and the assessments of human analysis. They lack the will to change or challenge the limitations placed upon them by themselves and others, and thus fail to take the necessary steps to develop their potential.[2]

Living your best life

What are these steps to developing one's potential? I pondered upon this question, and suggest that these steps are unique to each person. The issue is never how well we stand up in comparison to the rest of the world, but whether we are fulfilling our capability. It is all about being the best that you can be, or to put it in another way, about living your best life.

A TV documentary I once watched illustrates this very point. The topic was deaf-blindness and the development of a system of alphabets that enables deaf-blind people to communicate through touch. One gentleman said that he listened with his hands, he communicated with his hands, and he saw with his hands.

How did he develop what to most of us seems an impossibility? How do you listen and see with your hands? The ability to communicate in this manner was the bridge towards a life of maximised potential within this man's own circumstances.

The grandmother of a 12-year-old deaf and blind boy describes his journey as a series of achievements; each one, no matter how little, provides the strength to go on to reach for another one.

One step at a time, and each step we take brings us closer to who God made us to be.

For me, the process of developing my potential involved taking a close look at myself, identifying my talents, interests, likes and dislikes, and then taking the practical steps towards their development. This incorporates career, family, ministry or church-related functions, and social interests.

Failure is not a reason for me to stop; it has now become a reason to strive. It is never a question of how many times you have fallen, but whether you will pick yourself up and try again. It is understanding that the journey may be longer, but get there I will! One phrase has been instrumental in my journey. As my life unfolded, there were many times that I was anxious and a little fearful. There seemed to be many challenges, and on numerous occasions what lay ahead was very daunting; I did not feel that I had what was required. Then I heard Joyce Meyer, Christian best-selling author and motivational speaker, say something that in a sense set me free. Talking about her life and the challenges that she faced in the early days of her ministry, she said, 'I just do it afraid.' Rather than allow herself to be paralysed by fear, so that she was in a sense robbed of what God had planned for her future, she would keep going regardless of how she was feeling. 'Do it afraid,' she said. It did not matter how terrified she was, she would simply keep going. That is exactly how I have embarked on each new phase and how I still face each new challenge. I was afraid then, and I still am very often afraid; it is not headline news, and I doubt that this feeling will disappear any time soon. But I can choose to keep going regardless and continue to 'do it afraid'.

As I look back over the years, I realise that I am who and what I am today by the grace of God. By His grace I am qualified as a lawyer in two jurisdictions; I practised criminal law for several years, and recently began a new phase of life in a senior management position at a UK charity. By His grace I am an ordained minister of religion, with various opportunities to encourage others by the story of my life and the life-changing message of the gospel. By His grace I am in a good marriage which is strengthened day after day; we have been blessed with two wonderful children who are a continual reminder of God's faithfulness. Also by His grace I am discovering and rediscovering talents. I am a competent artist and have discovered a passion for hymn-writing and for story-telling. I have been able to influence, impact and encourage others, simply by being honest and open about my struggles and triumphs.

Day by day, it seems that I am becoming acquainted with the new me, which paradoxically is the 'old' or the 'original' me. It is the me that Jesus sees. It is the me that can do the 'impossible' when I reach for His strength, it is the me that is not limited by my past and my circumstances, and who can embrace tomorrow with confidence because I know that He is already there waiting for me.

Christ was secure; secure in who He was and in His purpose on earth. This security brought about a confidence and authority in the way He handled life's challenges and in His dealings and relationships with other people. As Christians, He now lives in us, and one of the benefits of having a relationship with Him is that we can access His security and allow it to overcome our fears and insecurities. We are new creations in Christ Jesus, 'old things are passed away'.[3] We can therefore actively bring about the daily renewal of our new selves.

Every day is another opportunity to strive for greater heights and make progress on that path towards attaining His purpose for my life.

You have a message

I have come to realise that we are being prepared for something. Every circumstance that we experience is woven into the strands of our lives. It may not look like it sometimes, but there is always a plan. Each person's life tells a story with a message attached to it. The issue is that we very often fail to recognise the value in our stories.

The first time that someone told me I had a message, I collapsed in giggling fits. 'God does have a sense of humour,' I thought. The next time someone told me that my life was a message that needed to be told, my laugh was halting and wrapped up in fear and panic. What sort of message could I possibly have? Was this a prelude for me being placed in a situation which required me to be out in the open?

Sometime afterwards, a leader of our children's church asked me to help her develop a mini seminar for churches to grapple with the issue of disability and how it is addressed in black majority churches. She wanted me to share my story as one of the speakers. I remember my hesitation. I had never spoken publicly about my life and I was not sure that it was something I could do. I tried to stall, but things started moving quite rapidly. I was surprised by the interest that had been generated in the other churches, and before long the day arrived.

The conference was an eye-opener for me. It brought home what I had suspected for a long time, that there was still stigma and shame attached to disability amongst ethnic groups. I knew that amongst Africans, disability was something that was hidden away. I was aware that culture and superstition were powerful forces, but surprised that cultural perceptions of disability still existed to the extent that people revealed that day.

What surprised me most was the fact that the Church, where people were supposed to find acceptance, was one of the places where discrimination was rife. I spoke candidly about my life and about the challenges that I had faced growing up. Others also opened up about their own experiences. The issues that were highlighted that day were complex. There was a lack of awareness of disability within a community that also struggled with the issue of denial. This sometimes stemmed from the erroneous belief that there was a cause attached to disability, and that its continued existence was indicative of something blameworthy on the part of the disabled person or their family.

Many people told stories of exclusion and isolation. Parents told stories of being admonished for their child's 'bad behaviour', and of some children being kept away from other children. We found out that people living with disability often feel invisible, and that there is little opportunity for full participation in church life. They encountered barriers everywhere, visible and invisible.

As I had researched the subject, I learned that it was a problem that is not limited to one particular community, but is more widespread.

During the interactive session, we discovered a common thread in all the stories; there was pain, frustration, but also determination. As each person spoke, something stirred in my heart. That old abhorrence of injustice and inequality rose up. I thought it was not right that people's experience of the Church was not as the haven that it was supposed to be. That day the seed was sowed and embedded in my heart, and I knew that I just had to do something. It was as though I was given a new set of eyes. I started seeing all the areas where we could make a difference just by making little changes – simple things we could do to make our churches more inclusive communities. I understood 'inclusive' to mean a welcoming environment where people felt able to approach others and form relationships, where everyone, regardless of their circumstances, could find their place alongside others and thrive in a safe environment.

I concluded that an initial, and perhaps the biggest, barrier was people's mindsets on the subject of disability. Breaking down mindsets involves lots of conversations, raising awareness, and recognising and confronting prejudices on both sides of the table. I knew that it was likely to be a long process.

I hoped that this first meeting would be the start of the conversation that would lead us to what Jesus intended His Church to be. The message that I hoped we would be sending out could be distilled into three simple phrases: open doors, open hearts, open arms.

As I thought about what to do and how to do it, I found help – lots of it. There were people who cared for or knew someone with a disability, people who had an interest, and people who lived with disability. We began brainstorming, and before long we were planning a disability awareness drive.

Doing it afraid

Each time I think that God is done with me, I realise that He is only giving me an opportunity to catch my breath! I left legal practice in 2010 and began working with the church in early 2013. In September of the same year, some months into my new role , I was part of a four-person team that participated in a three-day learning community with a range of other churches from the UK and Europe. It was a two-year commitment with the churches coming together every six months in the most breathtaking surroundings. It was a very diverse mix, and I was curious to discover how other people 'do church'.

The day usually started with a 15-minute time of devotion when someone gave an inspirational talk ending in prayers; each church took turns to lead these morning devotions. Soon it came round to my team, and to my horror I discovered that I had been 'nominated' to lead the session. I was awake for a large chunk of the night before, going over endless times what I would say and how I would say it. I was a ball of anxieties; I worried about the microphone playing up. I needed a hands-free microphone, and even though the organising team had assured me that they had this covered, I worried nonetheless. I worried about getting tongue-tied, I worried about letting my team down, I worried about not connecting with people, and I worried about making a complete fool of myself.

Eventually I did what I now consider to be the smartest and most productive thing that night. 'HELP ME, LORD!' I yelled into the dark. I don't know if it was His answer to my cry for help, but very soon afterwards I fell into the deepest, dreamless sleep.

My eyes snapped open a few hours later.

'I'm still here. I guess this means I have to go through with it!' I thought, extricating my limbs from the bedclothes.

I got dressed and made a poor pretence of trying to eat breakfast. Soon I was back in our meeting room. It was time.

As he snapped on my mic, the worship leader explained that he would sing a few songs first.

'I'll take my cue from you,' he said. 'You just let me know where you would like to land.'

'On my feet, hopefully!' I replied with a wry smile.

His laughter settled my nerves a little.

Almost too soon I was before the group. I looked up at expectant faces. I could make out smiles and heads bobbing up and down, encouraging me. We had bonded over the last year, but I was one of the less vocal members of the group. I started speaking. I talked about how special we each were to God, and how I expect Him to visit me each day, and consciously looked for Him as a result. I had had an interesting experience the previous day which I shared with the group.

The venue had huge grounds, and to help guests get around, the hotel had laid on a fleet of hackney carriages to transport guests from one place to the other. There was a range of wildlife on the grounds, including a large number of grouse. At the time I was on my way back to my room, which was situated a distance away from the meeting rooms, seated in the back of this quaint green hackney carriage. I stared out of the side window, lost in my own thoughts. We were chugging along at a snail's pace, when suddenly we came to an abrupt stop. I looked up. Before us was a silly-looking bird shambling across our path, slow and somewhat unsteady, obviously in no hurry. There were others of the same family on the grassy knoll to one side of the road. The driver apologised for the delay, but it was clear that these creatures were some sort of revered species. What were they? Pheasants? Grouse? Peacocks? (I later discovered that they were grouse!) As I sat staring at this spectacle, I distinctly heard a voice say: 'I will always wait for you. You are important enough for Me to stop everything just for you.'

'Woooo....' I thought. 'I have just been given a message through this ridiculous bird.'

There was something hugely comforting about this experience. What I found most heartwarming was the fact that God is always there, always letting me know that I am special, that He is attentive. He always knows where I am. Leading the devotion that morning, I coined a word of my own as I talked of my 'specialness'.

I ended with a prayer, eyes shut tight. There was a brief moment when you could have heard a pin drop, before the room erupted in applause. I opened my eyes slowly. I was sure you could see shock written all over my face. Somehow I made my way back to my seat before my trembling legs gave way. I sank into the chair. I could feel the tension slowly seep out of my pores.

'Thank You, Lord,' I whispered. 'You've covered my nakedness once again!'

A little later we broke for lunch. I had just sat down and was about to take a bite of my salad when one of the ladies came up to me.

'I'm sorry to interrupt your lunch. I wasn't in the room when you spoke this morning, but my husband just told me about your session.'

In my wildest dreams I could not have anticipated what she said next.

'We were wondering whether you would be willing to travel outside London ...'

I almost choked. A sound like something a half-strangled bird would make came out of me. It seemed that she may have interpreted this to mean a negative. She seemed so apologetic for interrupting my lunch.

When I recovered my composure I said, 'Oh yes, I do travel out of London.'

She continued. 'We were wondering whether you would speak at our women's conference.'

She said something about hoping my diary was not full, and hoping that I would be willing to accept the invitation to speak at their next women's conference in a year's time!

It is a good idea we are not mind-readers. Had she been able to see into my mind she would have seen amusement and confusion jumbled up in twisted knots. 'Speak at a women's conference… what next? God definitely has a sense of humour and I must be the subject of someone's mirth!'

'Erh, yes… ehm,' I stuttered, wondering what was happening to my tongue. For some reason it was not responding to commands.

I cleared my throat and started again.

Yes, I was happy to travel outside London (it turned out that their church was in the West Midlands). Yes, it would be my deepest honour to accept their invitation to speak at the conference.

She said she would send in a formal invitation when we all returned home, thanked me, and returned to her table.

'Did I just imagine that, Lord? What are you up to?' I asked silently. It all seemed like a dream. I kept shaking my head, expecting to wake up sometime soon.

Butterflies had already begun to do a slow waltz across my stomach.

'A conference? What on earth would I say to the people?'

Panic. More panic. My piece of ham which once had looked so appetising became rubber as I chewed on it.

A familiar voice whispered to my heart: 'Do it afraid!'

---

[1] John Mason, *You're Born An Original; Don't Die a Copy*, Oklahoma, Insight International, 1991).

[2] Myles Monroe, *Releasing Your Potential* (Shippensburg, PA: Destiny Image Publishers, 1997).

[3] 2 Corinthians 5:17, NKJV.

Chapter eleven
Finding meaning in adversity

Strength is gathered on the journey, not granted at the outset.
(Jared Brock[1])

We awaited Jedidiah's arrival with great expectation, but for me also with great trepidation. My feeling of anxiety was not helped by our history, which was challenging. Jedidiah was our fourth pregnancy, and the age gap between him and his sisters would be nine and 11 years respectively. Bajo and I had always wanted a house full of noisy children. Growing up with two brothers and two sisters, life was never dull, and I wanted to give our children the opportunity to experience all the joys of family as I had experienced. I always said, 'Two children are too few.' Our girls were exposed to the delights of family relationships, and they loved getting together with our extended family. They too were awaiting Jedidiah's arrival. Each day they would wiggle my tummy and say a few words to him. We included him in our prayers, and we talked about him and planned for him. They were not burdened by any fears that things might go wrong because they just did not know.

After Rinnah's difficult birth, it took us a long time to recover and for the sense of anxiety to fade. The last thing I wanted was to go through the trauma of pregnancy and childbirth all over again. We continued life, and I continued growing in my faith. Although I wanted more children, the idea of pregnancy terrified me, but I could not shake that gnawing feeling that my fear was keeping me from enjoying the fullness of what was freely available in Christ. This fear was so strong that I would shudder sometimes when I had flashbacks to my previous experiences of pregnancy. The only thing that made all the angst worthwhile was having the girls.

As I matured in my walk with the Lord, I began to feel very uncomfortable about an area in my life which showed what I recognised as a clear lack of trust. I reasoned that there was an increased chance that we would experience the same challenges in a future pregnancy, and I therefore thought it was likely that we were only meant to have these two children. In truth, I was more than happy with the girls if I knew that this was what God had planned for us, but I was not sure of that. I could not say that God had said, 'You are only to have these two children.' Each year as Rinnah got older I became even more restless about this area of my life that showed doubt in God's power. It was the wrinkle in my relationship with God, and it troubled me. I began praying about it, and for many months asked the Lord to 'help my unbelief'.[2] More time went by, and I finally got to the stage where I felt that I was strong enough to walk the pregnancy path. Bajo was well ahead of me; he had felt for some time that it was something we had to do, but he was waiting for me. One night he said: 'Baby, let's try for another little person. God will see us through.' It took me almost a full year before I said: 'OK. Let's do it.'

Weeks later we were pregnant, but we kept it quiet. I was not yet ready for the spotlight to be shone on me. At 12 weeks, we went for our first scan. I was excited, but also apprehensive. Old memories flooded back. The sonographer was very chatty and asked the usual questions: 'How old are your other children? Are you excited? Do you know what you would like?'

I muttered in response, hoping she would not be so chatty and would get on with things. Bajo, in his typical manner, was very curious and responded happily to her questions, throwing in several of his. I heard the squelch of the gel and felt its coldness against my skin. She applied some pressure with the foetal doppler and began moving it up and down. A few seconds passed. The atmosphere in the room changed. There seemed to be a cold chill which I was sure was not there when we arrived. She became very quiet, a frown cut across her forehead, and she stared intently at the monitor. She told us that she would be back in a minute and went out very quickly, returning almost immediately with her colleague. Bajo and I could do nothing but glance at each other. He grasped my hand and I squeezed tightly. There was no chatting this time. The second lady went through the same process. They exchanged looks.

I was very quiet. I had enough experience with medical personnel to know when there was a problem. I could read the signs well. And I did not care to know whatever it was that they could see on that grainy image on the screen.

'What is the matter?' Bajo asked.

'We can't detect a heartbeat… but sometimes this is not unusual,' the sonographer added quickly. 'We are going to perform a different kind of scan which will give us more information,' she told us, eyes still staring at the screen.

I did not need another scan to tell me what I had feared.

The baby had died.

'When it happens early on, this is sometimes the body's way of dealing with a problem in a pregnancy,' said the first lady very quietly.

I stared at the ceiling. I had this weird feeling that I was watching someone else's life play out in my presence.

They said they would leave us alone and encouraged us to take as long as we needed.

'What good will this do?' I thought. I could lay on that bed for the entire day and it would not change anything.

I wanted to get as far away as possible from the antenatal clinic. Bajo and I were out of there in minutes. We sat in the car park for ages, not saying anything, lost in our individual thoughts. I wondered whether we had made a mistake, and eventually I said as much.

'No,' he replied. 'We did not make a mistake. We heard God.'

I was not so sure that he was right.

'If we heard God, how come we are here?' my head screamed, but I said nothing.

Two weeks passed, which included an overnight hospital stay for me, and then I was back at work, living the routine of the past.

One morning I turned to Bajo and said: 'What now?'

He knew exactly what I meant.

'The plan has not changed,' he said. 'I don't know why we lost this baby, but it changes nothing. God is still God, and He will see us through as He has countless times before.'

Three months later, we were pregnant again. I felt a connection with this baby that I had not had with the other one. Like his sisters before him, I knew that he was a boy long before a scan told me so. Also, like his sisters, I had been given a name from the Lord for him. Excitedly, I told Bajo about how the name had come to me.

'Jedidiah', he mouthed, echoing my words. 'I like that.'

We shortened his name to Jed. We never referred to him as 'the baby', he was always 'Jedidiah'.

'This time will be different,' I kept telling myself, and I believed it.

The weeks went by, and I began to relax. I could feel the tension seep out of my body, and I began to plan for his arrival without a sense of foreboding. For years I had worked at my high-pressure job, overseeing some very high-profile criminal cases. I was tired, stressed out, and desperate for a break. I had also begun to get very restless about practising law. I was not sure that this was what I wanted to do for the rest of my life. I knew that I wanted to do something else, but I did not know what. Also, it seemed like a huge luxury to think about walking away from a career that had been built over many years when I had responsibilities and no trust fund! So when we became pregnant I looked forward to my maternity leave, which I hoped would give me the opportunity to exhale and plan for the future, and perhaps explore other areas of interest. Several people asked me what I was going to do. My response was always, 'I am going to explore my creativity!' I looked forward to days writing, and painting still life, and anything else that caught my fancy. I could not remember the last time that I had held a paintbrush in my hand, and I wanted to rediscover the joys of art.

Both our girls had arrived early and without warning, and I had left work unprepared, long before my intended leave date. I was determined that I would not be caught out if Jedidiah decided to go the same way. So I worked feverishly from the moment I attained 20 weeks, trying to get my caseload to where one of my colleagues could take over without too much trouble.

At 23 weeks I noticed I was getting out of breath. A visit to the GP resulted in a trip to Accident and Emergency and the beginning of a nightmare. There was no question about me returning home. Bajo went home to pack a bag of essentials and to try to explain to the girls where I was. For days I was subjected to a barrage of tests whilst the doctors tried to determine what the problem was. Before long they returned with a very scary diagnosis: heart failure. Apparently my heart muscles had weakened over a long period, following problems from when I was pregnant with Rinnah. There were no visible signs, no indicators that anything untoward might be bubbling beneath the surface. I was very active and enjoyed playing squash; I had a busy schedule and was very seldom ill. But it would have worsened progressively without treatment. This present pregnancy had triggered it and explained my shortness of breath, but it had also revealed the problem. Had I not been pregnant, it would have continued to get worse without any outward signs. I was like a walking time bomb. We were told by the doctors that it was a problem that could be fixed, but the drugs that were required were not safe to be used in pregnancy.

In view of the circumstances, there was the real possibility that Jedidiah would be delivered early, and the medical personnel were very twitchy because the hospital did not have a Special Care Baby Unit that could care for a baby that young. I remembered how tiny Rinnah was at 30 weeks, and I knew that a birth at 23 weeks was not good. Over the next few days, there were frantic calls to hospitals all over the south of England as the doctors searched for one that could accommodate Jedidiah and me. I was caught up in the worst nightmare ever, only it did not seem to have an end. I clung desperately to the Lord in those dark, dark days.

'Lord, I know You are there. Please help me.'

I was falling apart, and I feared that Bajo would soon start to unravel under the pressure of juggling a full-time job and trying to manage our household and two children who could not understand why they had not seen me for days. Risachi had just started secondary school, and I was heartbroken that I could not ease her through this major change.

On day five, we were told that a hospital in central London was prepared to receive me, and I was loaded into an ambulance for the 45-minute drive. Bajo drove behind the ambulance. Although it was one of the most frightening experiences of my life, I don't think I fully appreciated how dire the situation was. This was a blessing in itself. When we arrived at the hospital I was startled when I was wheeled through double doors above which appeared in large bold letters 'CRITICAL CARE UNIT'. I remember thinking, 'Am I in the right place?'

That first day I was visited by a steady stream of doctors, hooked up to all sorts of strange-sounding machines that flashed an array of colours, and a cocktail of medication was pumped into me at regular intervals. The nightmare continued. I shook my head often, hoping that this simple act would somehow help to restore order to my confusing situation. Something soon became apparent to me. It was unlikely that I was going to get to full term, and it was also unlikely that I was going to be let out to return home.

Days passed. No one talked about when I might be discharged, and I stopped asking. Each day I was taken down three floors to have an ultrasound scan. On the third visit, the doctor explained that there were concerns that Jed was not growing like he should. The more Bajo and I heard, the more we prayed. We got very little encouragement from our surroundings. I counted the days and prayed. I prayed and counted the days. Time passed slowly. I looked towards the end, even though it was nowhere in sight. I worried about the girls and tried to imagine a future when this particular storm would be over and we would be living a normal, uneventful life. But the future was very hazy, like trying to see through fog. I clung to God and talked to Jed, urging him to grow so we could go home.

'Hang in there, Jed,' I would whisper several times during the day. I told him about his sisters, and how they were waiting eagerly to welcome him home.

One afternoon, I remember that it was a Wednesday at the end of September, a midwife arrived to check the baby's heart rate. This was done every day, sometimes up to three times a day, and I hated the entire process. I hated the moments until they detected the baby's heartbeat. Today the chatter died down as she twisted and turned the monitor. She moved it up and down, pressing hard. Too hard.

'Sorry, sometimes they move about and hide away.'

'Déjà vu,' I thought.

After what seemed like an eternity, her machine detected a faint *thump-thump- thump*. Relief flooded her face, but it was short-lived. The sound began fading away again. She said that sometimes those little machines were not the most effective and she would get a better one with a screen attached.

She returned quickly with a doctor in tow wheeling a mobile machine.

'Déjà vu,' I thought again. 'Been here before!' My head screamed out.

Where was Bajo? Still more silent screaming in my head. I bit down hard on my lips, as though to keep the screams from jumping out of my mouth. Time stood still.

They went through the motions again, only this time we had a picture on the screen to go with the sound. I could see Jed's heart beating rapidly. It had no specific rhythm. Just an erratic bouncing on the screen and a low swishing then gurgling sound. Then as we watched, it began to slow. I stared, transfixed, terrified at what I was seeing, but unable to tear my eyes away.

Then it stopped altogether. And then there was a slight movement, a flicker as though he was fighting to stay alive.

'We need to get you down to the labour ward,' said the doctor urgently.

Everything became a blur, and I was transferred very quickly into a wheelchair and wheeled down several ramps to the labour ward. Now my thoughts seemed to be stuck like a needle in the old vinyl records of my youth. One phrase was playing over and over:

'Déjà vu!'

'Déjà vu!'

'Déjà vu!'

I noticed that Bajo had appeared. I was helped on to the bed, and a doctor went through the same motions as had been done a few minutes earlier. The room filled up with different people whose faces wore identical furrows in their foreheads. I found a spot on the ceiling and fixed my gaze on it.

Muffled sounds. Hushed tones.

Someone was speaking. It took several seconds for his words to permeate my consciousness.

'I'm sorry,' he said.

Time was suspended. My eyes had moved, following an invisible path from the ceiling, and now were fixed on his hands.

'What small hands for a man,' I thought.

Someone tapped my arm lightly, and I lifted my gaze and blinked to focus.

'I'm sorry,' he repeated. 'The baby's heart has stopped beating.'

'Déjà vu.'

'Déjà vu.'

'Déjà vu.'

The record screeched on.

I stared at him, wondering why he was whispering, why the group circling me was staring intently at me. I heard his words, but I was having difficulty comprehending. I experienced a terrifying sense of bilocation: one person, a detached and calm observer, watching this other person.

'Pull yourself together,' I urged myself.

Panic was gnawing at the edges of my mind, threatening my composure. I realised that they were waiting for a response from me, but I did not know how to respond. What do you say in the moment when you are faced with the reality of shattered hopes? I instinctively placed my hand on my stomach; a mother's protective instinct, as though that simple gesture would somehow ward off the horror of those words. My next thought was a question directed at the doctor.

'How do you know? You are not God.'

Perhaps he could read the defiance in my eyes; he turned to my husband and began explaining to him what had happened, how it was not entirely unexpected, given the complications that I had had over the last few weeks.

This was my third week in hospital, and week 27 for Jedidiah. We had one more week to go before he was to have been delivered at 28 weeks.

One week.

Seven days.

So close. And yet so far.

Each new day had brought us closer to that goal. Each morning, Bajo would call me before he got the girls ready for school, and we would thank the Lord for another day. That morning had been no different, and I could not comprehend how a day that had started with such promise was to end with such tragedy. I felt like a child who had been given a much-

149

expected Christmas gift and then had had it wrenched viciously from their grasp just as they were about to open it.

I stared blankly ahead, catching snippets of their conversation.

'... safer to induce labour.'

'... last anything up to 36 hours.'

Soon the room emptied, and Bajo and I were left alone to reach a decision on what to do, whether we wanted the baby to be delivered by Caesarean section or whether labour was to be induced. The doctors were keen for us to opt for inducing labour because of the additional complications involved in a Caesarean birth and the risk that it posed for me. They had stepped outside to give us time to allow things to sink in.

Now there was no rushing about; we had all the time we needed to make a choice, which was really no choice.

C-section. Dead baby.

Labour induced. Dead baby.

Bajo had switched into a functional mode. His face was expressionless, and I knew that he would be thinking about how best to take charge of the situation.

'Baby, we can't have a Caesarean,' he said gently. 'I'm not risking you. We have to think about the girls.'

He was right. But the other option filled me with dread.

'How can I go through labour just to give birth to a dead child? How do I get through that?' I whispered, still feeling as though I was trapped in a nightmare and unable to rouse myself.

'God will see us through.' His voice was strong, and like so many times in the past, I drew strength from his strength.

'God will see us through,' he repeated.

God will see us through

Labour was long and agonising. I was no stranger to pain, but this was indescribable. Both our girls had been born early by Caesarean section, and I had never before experienced labour. Now it seemed like the cruellest of blows to endure all that suffering for the first time with nothing to show for it at the end.

Our son was born two days later, as dawn ushered in a new day. I was shaken by the silence and the stillness of the atmosphere.

'Babies are supposed to cry,' my heart screamed.

The room ought to be filled with the sound of voices.

'Look, it's a boy!'

'Dad, would you like to cut the cord?'

'Who does he look like?'

'He looks like me. He has my nose. How much does he weigh?'

'Let's call the girls and tell them that they have a little brother.'

The silence was deafening, eerie, and to me it appeared mocking. I found myself muttering, 'Yet will I praise Him.'

'Would you like to hold him?' asked the midwife, quietly breaking into my thoughts. She had been wonderful, and we had bonded during the long hours of this ordeal. She was due to go off shift at 6 a.m. but had assured me that she would not leave until Jedidiah was born. I had asked God to keep her there for me. Jedidiah's arrival half an hour to the end of her shift told me that He cared and was still taking care of the details.

'His dad will hold him,' I said.

Jedidiah was handed to his father, this child for whom we had waited for so long, the answer to prayers. He was so perfectly formed, yet so still, so silent. Bajo took him in his arms, named him, and then thanked God for choosing us to be his parents. I did not hold him, but Bajo sat in a chair next to me so I could see him clearly. I spent long moments looking at him, my heart filled with thoughts of what could have been. I saw in my mind's eye flashes of a future that would never be; Jedidiah smiling and stretching his arms up to me, him crying for Risachi to pick him up, taking his first step, and finally, on his first day at school. There the pictures ended.

He bore an uncanny resemblance to Bajo. In that moment my overriding feeling was of regret, but it was not a despair-filled regret. It was a quiet acceptance of something that was beyond my control, but alongside this was the awareness that this was not everything, that what we were seeing and experiencing was only part of a bigger or fuller picture. And I did not know what that full picture was yet.

I told Jedidiah that I would have loved to have been his mother for longer, but that I was giving him back to our Father. Together, Bajo and I returned Jedidiah to the safety of our Lord.

Much later on, after Jedidiah had been taken away and Bajo had gone to check on our girls, I had my first proper conversation with the Lord.

'I don't understand why Jedidiah didn't live, Lord, and I need Your help to get through this.'

There was nothing. No sound.

I continued.

'Lord, I feel very disappointed. I was all geared up to look after a baby. Now I don't know what to do with myself. I'm very confused. What do I do with my life now? What is the plan? I know You have one. I need You to tell me, please.'

Then one word popped into my mind, but it seemed to start out like a tiny thought, like a seed, and then it mushroomed and became stronger. Much like an echo it reverberated, on and on like rolling waves.

'Write.'

'WRITE.'

---

[1] Jared Brock, *A Year of Living Prayerfully: How a Curious Traveler Met the Pope, Walked on Coals, Danced with Rabbis, and Revived His Prayer Life* (Carol Stream, IL: Tyndale House, 2015).

[2] See Mark 9:24, NKJV.

Chapter twelve
A new season

The way to be with God in every season is to strive to be near
Him every week and each day.
(Thomas S. Monson, American clergyman[1])

The river of my life flowed into a new season with no specific
name, nothing that fitted into a definite box. After the
turbulence of the last few months I was driven to claw back
some control, and so I called this new season 'After Jedidiah' –
AJ. In the months AJ, I wrote and wrote and wrote some more.
I have always functioned best when I have some guidance and
focus. I still had no idea why we had to go through the
challenging months of pregnancy only to lose Jedidiah at the
end, but having a clear indication of what I was to do next
certainly made the months afterwards easier to get through. With
each day I was discovering that God's thoughts are so far
removed from our thoughts and sometimes His ways are beyond
our comprehension.[2] He promised that there would be good in
everything that happens to us.[3] Though I had questions, I was
happy to wait patiently for the good to emerge.

I did not know what to write, and so I wrote about any and
everything. I wrote for up to ten hours every day and was

surprised at what emerged. I wrote about everyday scenes; trips to the grocery store, the school run and my daily walk were the subject of my musings. I wrote about people I encountered every day; I wrote about biblical characters, placing them in today's setting. I let my imagination roll unrestrained, nothing was safe from my pen! I was certainly 'exploring my creativity'! Healing was a slow process, and I was in no hurry to get back into the rat race that had been my previous life.

As the day drew closer for my return to work at the end of my maternity leave, I knew that for the time being this life in the fast-paced, pressure-filled environment of a busy legal practice no longer featured in my short-term future. Very often it takes a traumatic experience to help us make the decisions that may have terrified us in the past. It takes being faced with the reality of your mortality for you to prioritise what is truly important and pursue how you want to spend the time that you have here. In that moment your vision is unclouded by the pressures and cares of life, and perhaps the clearest it has ever been.

I wanted to have a sense of 'building something' that I could hold in my hands, and writing gave me that. It was one of the most difficult things that I had ever attempted, and it required great discipline. But the sense of fulfilment that I felt at the end of a good day of writing was quite remarkable. Up to that point, no one outside my family had seen any of the writing, and I wanted to hear an independent opinion. I was curious to hear what someone without personal ties to me thought. I enrolled on a creative writing course at a local university, and was immediately immersed in a new and exciting world. One day we had an assignment on which the class was to provide feedback. I decided to try my hand at poetry, even though it would be the first poem that I had written since my schooldays.

After much thought I settled on a subject which with hindsight was quite unusual, considering the setting and audience. As I wrote, I was surprised by the ease with which words flowed from my head. I could not believe what was taking place. My fingers flew across my keyboard, tapping vigorously. My breath was trapped somewhere between my lungs and my throat as I feverishly tried to keep pace with the avalanche of words that tumbled out from an unknown source. I was afraid to stop just in case I could not return to this place that I had never before experienced. When the surge was over, these words were left on the screen:

Bruised, battered, beaten and broken
Robes tattered and torn, blood and sweat mingled,
Crimson stains on purple, stripped and striped
Mocked by a baying crowd, not a word uttered aloud
Are you the one, O King? Defend yourself, O King
Still, not a sound spoken by tongue
The masses, as evil distilled, with one voice instilled
Crucify! Crucify! But why? O why?
Yet not a sound spoken by tongue
Hope all at once appeared so lost?

Thirty-three years past on one clear night
A lone star shines to mark the spot,
A baby born in humble form, hope borne on shoulders young
A carpenter's son, in truth with lofty pedigree
From cheeky boy to confident man grew
For three and a half His name we knew.
Thick scales from covered eyes drop
Limp limbs like oak trees stand
Voices once lost with a pop are found
Joy, joy, unspeakable joy.

But now in one fell swoop
Darkness descends like a blanket thick

Flowing tears like a swirling flood
Hearts torn, Hope hangs in tattered shreds
And like a stone from heaven plummets
Hope descends to depths so deep.
But wait! Hush now
A new day peeps,
Hope once lost from ashes ascends
And Joy forevermore is ours to keep.[4]

The following day I was stunned by the positive reaction of what was a very mixed bunch that expressed opinions without reservation. I was humbled, deeply humbled, and wondered what else lay within. Buoyed by this small victory, I wrote more poetry and one day decided to attempt some hymn-writing. I was on a voyage of discovery; it was my time to unfurl. My curiosity was piqued. I was just as much of an observer as anyone watching from the outside, as my life unfolded. It was like opening up one of those chocolate assortments in the shiny wrapper without having studied the packaging to find out what lay inside. Each one a different shape, size and texture. Slowly you separate the chocolate from its shiny covering and pop it into your mouth. You bite down and there is immediately an explosion of flavour: brandy, vanilla, and caramel, a gooey stream oozing out and surprising the eater. The joy of the eating was partly in the mystery of the unknown and the experience of opening the coloured wrapper and discovering what was in it. Writing was like that for me. I did not know what I would find when I bit into it. And as time went on, I was surprised, pleasantly so.

Ten months after I began this literary journey, I had the first draft of a work of fiction. I continued writing, and produced a series of short stories. I wrote some more; a collection of different pieces on a range of diverse and unrelated subjects came to life. My family began urging me to get something published.

'Baby, I love reading everything you write, but I don't think God gave you these ideas just for me,' Bajo said, ever the voice of reason.

'Hmm... ' I replied, leaving him to figure out what this meant.

I did nothing to try to get my work published, because I was not ready for the exposure. I tried to explain this to him once, and I talked about the vulnerability of having strangers examine your work, and the awareness that there would no longer be a hiding place. His baffled look said he did not understand at all, but he said nothing. He continued to give me space to write, continued to read everything that I produced, proffering his thoughts, suggestions and encouragement. He never put pressure on me, but instead began researching agents and publishers.

After a while, I reached an agreement with the Lord. I said, 'Lord, I will work hard. I will write whatever You ask me to write, but You decide what You want to do with it. I promise that when You open the doors, I will be ready.'

I continued writing, and one day, as I mentioned above, I thought I might try writing a hymn. Whilst I was in hospital in the long weeks before Jedidiah was born, a dear friend had visited and brought with her a book on hymns and the writers behind the popular songs that we sing today. I had read their stories and been moved by the experiences that had been catalysts for such moving songs. I was listening to the 'The Old Rugged Cross', a popular hymn written sometime in 1912 by American evangelist and song-leader George Bennard (1873– 1958), when the idea popped up in my head... 'Why don't you write a hymn?'

'Hmm… not a bad idea,' was my response. 'But I've never written one before. I don't know how.'

'It's sort of like a poem. Why don't you try?' came the reply.

'But who will put music to it?' I asked.

'One step at a time. Write it first.'

And so I set to work writing. I thought that I would try to write something each day, and that if I got enough songs, perhaps I could publish a little book of hymns. The working title 'A Hymn a Day' emerged, and I wrote the first hymn early one morning with the breaking dawn as my inspiration.

My God Who Forgives
Create in me a clean heart, O Lord.
Cleanse me through with Your pure Word.
Though wretched sinner that I am,
Myself, the world and I condemn,
You are to me, my God-Who-Forgives.

Though time and talent I did squander,
Down crooked paths my feet did wander,
With dark thoughts my mind is cluttered,
And twisted words my lips have uttered,
Still You remain, my God-Who-Forgives.

Your sweet words like soothing balm,
To desperate heart You whisper calm,
While raging storms do toss and roll
And life's mistakes exact their toll,
Forever You are my God-Who-Forgives.[5]

After about a year, I had the drafts of four books and had worn off the letters on the keypads of two laptops with my incessant tapping away. I began to get a sense that change was imminent, although I had no idea what it might be. One day in September 2012, I was approached by the senior pastor of my church with an offer to come into the church and oversee the office. My first reaction was laughter. I pointed out the fact that I was a solicitor with no management experience besides running a criminal litigation department. I also told him that I was not looking for employment, but even as I said those words I had a funny feeling that this would be my next assignment.

'Pray about it,' he said, leaving me with my jumbled thoughts.

When I told Bajo about the offer, he nodded mysteriously and said, 'It all makes sense.'

I asked him what made sense, but he only said, 'We'll pray about it.'

I looked back over the last few months and I saw that in reality the Lord had been preparing us for this time. Just a few days earlier, we had taken our girls to their new school. They were settling down and the home front was sorted out, leaving me free to take on new challenges knowing that they were safe. This was an opportunity to reinvent myself. As far as I was concerned, it was something that came out of the blue, which was not on my career path. But I was soon to realise that everything I had done previously would find a place in this new role. Even seemingly trivial positions in my past had given me experience and skills which I found to be relevant.

For many years, I had craved a sense of 'building something', and I realised this was finally being satisfied. The work was challenging but fulfilling. It could be summed up in one phrase – 'changed lives'. It was about building relationships and impacting lives positively. I was grateful to be doing something which was clearly meaningful, and I threw myself into my work, but still dedicated one day to writing. I continued working simultaneously on various writing projects, and one book in particular soon emerged as a frontrunner. Not surprisingly, I thought that this would be the first book that would be published, and gave it all my attention.

One day, during our office meeting, we had an American visiting minister, Prophetess Francina Norman, address the staff. It was a busy time in the office and my mind had strayed to some of the work that I needed to oversee that morning. I glanced at my watch to see how much time was left of the hour. I was already sorting through in my head which issues I would tackle first. Prophetess Norman was rounding up. I was seated towards the front of the room, but she had walked down the aisle to the rear. She came back up and began what I thought was a closing prayer. Suddenly she walked towards me, stopped a few feet away and said, 'I just hear the Lord say that you've got to write this book. He says you've been procrastinating and you say, "Oh, I'm just too busy." But you have to write this book…'

I was stunned.

'Who could have told her? How could she possibly know things that she couldn't possibly know?'

Even in my surprise I thought, 'I wonder which book she is referring to.'

It was as though she could read my mind. Her next words left me in no doubt.

'… because the book is not only going to bring healing to other people but is going to bring healing to you. And God says you've got to do it; you've got to take the time and you have to do it. And it needs to be finished this year.'

She spoke of how much God had put in me from childhood, referring to me as a 'walking miracle'.

She concluded by asking everyone in the room to tell me to: 'Write the book!'

Everyone echoed, 'WRITE THE BOOK!'

'You've got no excuses now,' she said.

That was in July 2014.

When I got home that evening, I told Bajo about the entire staff meeting incident. He confirmed what I had figured out, that the book to which she referred was *Complete in Him*. The challenge was that I had all but forgotten about its existence. It was the very first proper book that I had attempted writing, over a decade before, and I had no clear idea where it was. I set about searching, frantically.

I had had a number of computers in the ten years, and although all my writing was transferred to each new laptop, the draft of *Complete in Him* was nowhere to be found. The closest I came to a result was the contents page saved in one of the folders. Over the next few weeks, I went through our home like a blizzard, looking through boxes and boxes of journals and all sorts of discarded material. I found lots of interesting, long-forgotten bits of writing, telling stories of their own. The process was slow because my attention kept drifting. After several hours of searching I was getting nowhere. I had hoped that I would find a hard copy tucked away somewhere in our study, and even though the thought of retyping pages and pages of text did not thrill me in the least bit, it was much better than having to rewrite the entire book.

I paused to regroup.

'Lord, help me find this book. You know where it is. Please show me where to look,' I whispered.

I continued wracking my brain, trying to figure out where I could have stashed it. And then it dawned on me. I always emailed each completed piece of writing to Bajo, and I was sure that I had emailed this to him as well. I told him what I was thinking, and he began a search of his various email accounts. I was looking over his shoulder, literally breathing down his neck. After a few minutes we saw an email pop up with an attachment titled *Complete in Him*. We both shouted in delight, but my enthusiasm was doused when I saw that there were only 45 pages of text. This was nowhere near completion. How could I possibly complete this book in a few short weeks? It was now the second week in August, and I had a deadline that was not of my making! And I had the feeling that there would be no negotiating on this. I was clearly in a race against time.

A race against time

I sat down with the draft which looked alarmingly slim. As I read, I noticed that my writing style had developed since I had first penned those words. I saw places where it was clear that rewrites were necessary. Also, ten years is a very long time, and so much had happened in our lives during that period. I knew that I had a lot of material that could be used, but I was still uncomfortable about writing about my life so openly. I was painfully aware that this was another hurdle that I had to overcome, but I was also very determined. If God had sent a prophetess across the 'pond' to deliver a message to me, then I would not let anything stand in the way of this.

I felt like I was walking in biblical times, maybe like a man called Jonah[6] who was off on his own tangent doing the opposite of what he had been instructed to do, until he was reined in. If I had to write my story, I thought the chapter would begin with these words:

> And the word of the Lord came to Chizor through the mouth of His prophet. 'Turn aside from your ways and complete the work that I have given you. Be of good courage for it is I that instructs you.' And Chizor repented of her ways and turned fully to the work of the Lord her God.

Over the next few weeks I wrote every waking moment. I survived on little sleep and saw everyday activities of life as unwelcome interruptions. I wrote through my lunchtime and in any spare moment. I wrote until the words danced before my eyes and my head felt like it was packed with cotton wool. Sometimes I would fall asleep with my fingers still on my keyboard, and Bajo would retrieve my laptop from folds of bedding. Sometimes I would wake up with sentences in my head and scramble for my journal so that I could capture them before they floated away. Early one morning at the end of October I felt that I had completed it. It was done… finally!

'I'm done!' I announced, nudging a sleepy Bajo.

It was a strange moment. I had anticipated it for so long. The emotions filtered through slowly. Adrenaline coursed through my veins, and butterflies flapped madly in my gut. I experienced another jumbled-up mix of feelings and emotions. The best description was of a freshly baked cake with a mishmash of flavours. You take a bite and try to identify the different flavours that burst through. That morning I recognised elation, excitement, incredible fatigue, and apprehension.

I had poured my heart and soul into this project for so long. It seemed that every moment that I could wrestle away from life I had tapped relentlessly at my keyboard. Word after word, forming sentences, paragraphs and chapters, my eye drifting regularly to the word counter in the corner of the screen. Now what? Like Bajo always reminded me, I had not written it for myself and a handful of others to read; it was now time to seek to release it into the world. The mere thought of my life laid out before innumerable eyes filled me with dread, but I was on some sort of a conveyor belt and powerless to stop it. And the truth was that even if I could stop, I would not. I had the unshakeable sense that I was walking destiny's path.

It was done. It was time for the big reveal!

You have in your hands the culmination of a dream that was 11 years in the making, but the story is not finished, for the journey continues. No matter what the future holds, I know that in Him, in our Lord Jesus, I am complete.

---

[1] Thomas S. Monson, '9/11 Destruction Allowed us to Spiritually Rebuild'. Onfaith blog, 8th September 2011. Available at http://www.faithstreet.com/onfaith/2011/09/08/911-destruction-allowed-us-to-spiritually-rebuild/11965 (accessed 21st September 2015).

[2] Isaiah 55:8.

[3] Romans 8:28.

[4] © Chizor Akisanya, 2011.

[5] © Chizor Akisanya, 2012.

[6] The complete story appears in the book of Jonah in the Bible.

Chapter thirteen
Complete in Him: the process of change

My weakness, that is, my quadriplegia, is my greatest asset
because it forces me into the arms of Christ every single
morning when I get up.
(Joni Eareckson Tada[1])

I cannot look over my life thus far and say that I have achieved
anything in my own strength. I consider my life, and my heart
wells up and bubbles over with gratitude. It has not been easy,
but God has lifted me above each challenge, far beyond my
expectations. I have had encouragement directly from Him,
through His written Word, and through those spoken to my
heart. He has placed different people in my path at key stages or
periods, people who have stood in my corner and willed me to
reach for higher heights. God has shown me that He is my
source, and that in Him there are no limitations on my ability to
achieve. I have found several contradictions in my life; it is when
I am at my most helpless that I have recorded some interesting
achievements.

I have put together a list of points that have helped me in the process of renewing my mind and changing my perception of myself. I hope that perhaps they encourage someone reading this book to challenge their present limitations, to make a commitment to change, and thus begin the process of realising their potential.

1. Do not imagine that your disability is the first thing that the world sees in you.

Even if it is impossible not to notice your disability, do not give the impression that it is what characterises you. In other words, do not act as though it is the most important thing about you. You are more than whatever your condition might be. You are a person first, and like everyone else you have gifts and talents. I had a very interesting experience not too long ago. It was not a new experience, it was something that I have encountered at different times in the past. I had met a lady several months ago. In the time that I have known her we have had several conversations, and my husband had invited her and her partner over to our house for dinner. On this particular day, we met and were exchanging pleasantries when she suddenly gasped. Hand clasped to her mouth, eyes wide open she blurted out, 'Oh my goodness, what have you done to your arm?'

Thinking it was a recent thing, she continued, 'When did it happen?'

Her outburst was dramatic and unexpected. Sometimes I am prepared for this reaction. This was not one of those times. It had been a long day, and my mind was on other matters. I tried to wave it away, but she thought that I had broken my arm or been the victim of something disastrous since the last time that I had seen her, only a few weeks earlier, and so she ploughed on.

Finally I said, 'It was a birth injury.'

Her cheeks caved in on themselves as realisation dawned on her. I saw embarrassment carve a path across her face.

'Oh my goodness. I'm so sorry, I didn't realise...'

'It's all right... really,' I said hastily, trying to reassure her and let her know that I was not offended.

It turned out that she had never noticed my arm. She was not the first person who said as much, and I doubt that she will be the last. Sometimes because things are obvious to us, we think that they must be obvious to others. But it may be the case that people don't see what we think is so obvious. Ask yourself this question: 'Who is the person behind the disability?' This is the person that we ought to present to the outside world.

2.   Do not use your disability as an excuse for not trying.
Sadly there are people who exploit their disability. There are people who rail against the world, seeking to blame others for their impairment. There are people who have a sense of entitlement. There are parents who use their child's disability as an excuse for bad behaviour. I have met some, although thankfully not many, who fall into one or more of these categories. I have also met people who for a variety of reasons have given up. Sometimes it is as a result of a lack of encouraging support, or it may be due to the fear of failure. Unfortunately, I have come to realise that there will always be 'nay-sayers' who believe that you cannot achieve. You may never be able to 'put prejudice to flight', for this is largely beyond your control. In all likelihood, you will experience ignorance; you may find yourself on a collision course with society's entrenched attitudes that place disability in a specific box. People will think what they want to think, but you have a choice – this means that you have to decide for yourself: do you want to be defined by other people's opinions or prejudices?

For me, it was very much a practical decision – if I don't give it a try, then I will never know. The thought of never knowing what is possible spurs me on. I constantly remind myself that life is not a dress rehearsal for the main event... this is it, this is show time! I cannot get back any time that I squander in procrastination, in fear or in discouragement. If I try and it does not work out, my comfort is this: at least I tried and I had the experience of doing so. Disability must never be disabling!

3.   Adopt a positive approach to/outlook on life.

A cheerful disposition acts like a magnet to the world. No one wants to be around a miserable, negative person. Someone said that the only disability in life is a bad attitude. A bad attitude is a bad attitude; you cannot sugar-coat it. I have met some people living with disabilities who had a sense of entitlement which was most unattractive. They behaved as though the world owed them for the situation that they were in. I was rather amused by a post I read somewhere about a disabled man on a motorised scooter who boarded a train, almost running over a fellow commuter's foot, did not bother to apologise, and then parked himself such that he blocked the aisle. Whenever he was asked to move so someone could get on, he gave them a withering look, tutted under his breath and inched forward a fraction, even though there was room ahead. Whilst people will usually excuse such behaviour because they think that the person has a lot on their plate, it does leave a bad taste in one's mouth.

I have also met others who had quite extensive disabilities and who radiated such warmth that drew people to them like a magnet.

I think that having an attitude that is not tainted by bitterness is a powerful and memorable message to the world. It will give you a voice that people want to listen to. Above all, it will give you an opportunity to talk about the love that God lavishes so freely on us.

> When you hear the word 'disabled,' people immediately think about people who can't walk or talk or do everything that people take for granted. Now, I take nothing for granted. But I find the real disability is people who can't find joy in life and are bitter.
> (Teri Garr, American actress and dancer, best known for her role in the 1980s comedy film *Tootsie*, who was diagnosed with multiple sclerosis.)[2]

4. Take advantage of the aids and assistive supports that have been developed to increase your quality of life.

When I was a child, I so desperately wanted to get to 18 years old so that I could drive. When I did get behind a wheel, it was clear that I needed some kind of adaptations fitted. I did not know where to turn. One day my sister came across some information on driving instructors for the disabled, and booked me in for my first lesson. It was a fantastic experience, and I loved every minute of it. I was introduced to a steering ball and infrared controls which meant that I could drive safely and competently with one hand. After a few months, I passed my test at the first attempt.

Just over a year ago, I got a new car and my husband took it in to a car adaptation company to be fitted with infrared hand controls. There had been various advances in technology since we had last purchased a driving aid, and we were both amazed by the different conversions that were possible to assist disabled drivers. Over the two days that it took to have the rewiring done, my husband spent some time with the gentleman who owned the business. He was moved by the owner's story of how he got into the car adaptation business. His wife had polio and he had adapted a car for her use. He was an engineer, and used his experience to design and fit hand controls with hydraulic links to the pedals of her car. I am one of thousands who have benefited and continue to benefit from the ingenuity of designers of products that have enhanced the quality of life for people living with disabilities.

It has been several years since I got my driver's licence, but today I still get a buzz whenever I get into my car. I never take driving for granted. I love the sense of independence that it gives me; I love the surprised look on people's faces when they see me get behind the wheel, and I am grateful for those inventions that make it possible for disabled people to function on an equal footing with everyone else.

5. Constantly expect healing, but in the meantime go about your life being and doing the very best that you can.

I have come across several Christians living with disabilities who seem to struggle with the notion of healing and faith on the one hand, and their circumstances on the other. Many of them are stuck in a place where they feel that any attempt to embrace assistance, medical or technological, is an indication of doubt and unbelief. Unfortunately, there are members of the Christian community who suggest that any deviation from a belief in the singular path that God *will* heal is an indication of a lack of faith. They tend to expect this healing to come in a very set way and reject anything that does not fit with their perception of healing. And so the result is people who refuse to take their medication, parents who deny their disabled children access to medical and physical assistance, people who refuse to take advantage of the support that is freely available. They say that they are 'believing God for their healing'. But the outworking of this is that their quality of life is very often diminished.

I say this very carefully, but there is a thin line between faith and irresponsibility, and I think that it is easy to slip into what might be a state of denial. I have never believed that making the most of practical and medical support is an indication of a lack of faith. God heals in countless ways and through countless means. Healing, when it comes, will be in His own time and in His own way.

When I made the decision that I would no longer accompany my mother on those trips to healing ministries in search of a cure, I was about 18 or 19 years old. I knew that it hurt her greatly, but I decided that I needed to concentrate on making the most of my life as it was at that present time; in a sense, I would concentrate on living my best life rather than live somewhere in the future. It was not a case of one path cancelling out the other. I was simply doing the best with what I had. I believe that Jesus heals, I have seen much evidence of this, but until He does, I can strive to maximise each moment of each new day. To do less would be showing a lack of appreciation for the amazing gift of life.

6. Learn to be comfortable in your own skin.
Be honest with yourself; do not be afraid to seek help – this is not a sign of weakness. Understand your present limitations, and gradually seek to extend those limitations (rationally). Set personal targets, goals and challenges, and reward yourself for each victory. Do not adopt other people's targets as yours, and never compare yourself to them.

I have found self-acceptance to be extremely liberating and empowering. Self-acceptance means taking a realistic look at yourself, saying, 'this is me'; it means learning and unlearning certain things. Learning to like yourself, learning to be comfortable with yourself and in your own skin, learning to see yourself as God sees you, learning to seek help and accept help when it is offered. It means unlearning self-criticism which strips away your self-esteem and reduces you as a person, unlearning the habit of comparing yourself to other people and of adopting other people's goals as yours. Trying to fit into other people's shoes is uncomfortable. They pinch and soon make walking unbearable. I am the only me there is, and nobody can be me as well as I can!

Mark Twain said: 'The worst loneliness is to not be comfortable with yourself.'[3]

Self-acceptance is not resignation, it is the foundation upon which you can begin to build. For me, it was a case of saying, 'This is where I am, this is what my challenge is. Now, how can I get from where I am to where I want to be?' It is living each day knowing that limitations can be redefined and that there is always a way through, over or around each challenge.

I am now no longer averse to asking for help if I need it. This did not come easily and I had to consciously practise until my discomfort eased away. When I go to the grocery store and I am asked at the checkout whether I need help, I will sometimes accept the offer even though I have mastered the art of packing up groceries with speed and efficiency. When people offer to carry my bags, I let them, and when I travel alone by air I will ask for help to place my hand luggage in the overhead bin.

I understand that everyone's journey is different. Whilst there may be various similarities, our journeys are suited for our circumstances and personalities. I reward myself for every victory, no matter how small it might be to someone else.

Whilst you are building your self-esteem, I have found that certain things help. Wear what suits you, wear what you are comfortable with, wear what flatters. Move at your own pace, never accept other people's standards as yours, and *never* judge your progress by other people's.

7. **Develop the positive attitudes that come from the personal experience of living with a disability; for instance, understanding, compassion, strength of character.**

One of the positive outcomes of going through or living with a challenge is developing an understanding of what someone else experiencing something similar might be struggling with. The struggles I faced as a young girl birthed in me a desire to help other young girls who might be experiencing similar challenges. As a result, I notice things and can begin conversations that may be awkward for someone else.

A few years ago I was at church, when my eyes rested on a girl in the congregation. She looked to be in her early 20s. I had not seen her before and I did not know who she was. I noticed her because she was standing awkwardly, and when she walked it was clear that there was a problem with her legs. I found out later that she had had double hip replacements. That day, as I looked at her I heard a voice say: 'Tell her not to worry, she will get married.' Startled, I glanced around, looking for the source of the voice. I heard the words again, only more insistent this time.

'She'll think I'm a nut!' I muttered.

But I went over to her regardless, and repeated the words. I was startled by her reaction. She burst into tears. I had no idea but she had been praying about her future and about her prospects of getting married, which she believed were non-existent because of her disability. I used myself as an example, and told her that God would surprise her. Today she is married with a family, and thriving.

I heard it said somewhere that whatever does not kill you will make you stronger.[4] (The actual quote is: 'That which does not kill us makes us stronger'.)

I think that the human spirit is extremely resilient and that we really have no idea how much we can bear until we go through a difficult situation. There is just something instinctive in us that abhors the thought of simply rolling over and dying. The Bible puts it this way: 'God…will not let you be tempted beyond what you can bear' (1 Corinthians 10:13, NIV UK, 2011). Whenever I am going through a tough time and I remember this verse of scripture, I mutter two things to myself. First, 'God obviously has more confidence in me than I have in myself!' And secondly, when my eyes open each morning and I find myself at the start of a new day, I think, 'Well, I'm still here, so I guess it means that I can bear this challenge a little longer!'

I don't think that there is anything remarkable about my journey. There are lots of people I have met or heard about who have faced far worse adversities than I have faced. Recently I came across a book about a woman who had lost a hand and an eye after walking into the propeller of a small plane. Lauren Scruggs was a fashion journalist and blogger who at 23 years old was poised on the cusp of opportunity and success when the accident occurred, altering her life dramatically and irrevocably. As she recovered, she thought she was ugly and that no one would ever love her, and that her life was ruined.

With family support and her Christian faith, she embraced her new life, her new normal. She believed that God has a specific purpose for her life and wanted to use her experiences to reach young girls.

I was so delighted to read about her marriage last December.

8. **Keep things in perspective. Remember that no matter how bad you think your situation may be, there is always someone worse off. Make a habit of being thankful.**

When I was a child, there was a song called 'Count Your Blessings' that we were taught at Sunday school. It was a popular hymn, but it was the chorus that has stayed with me after so many years. The lyrics were by Johnson Oatman, Jr (1856–1922), an American Methodist reverend who was one of the most prolific gospel song writers of the late nineteenth/early twentieth centuries. The lyrics encouraged us to count our blessings and if we did, we might be surprised by what God had done for us.

When we would sing with gusto, loud and out of tune and accompanied by a lone piano, it was just another one of those catchy tunes that characterised our Sunday school days. As an adult, it has acquired new meaning for me and helps me to maintain a healthy perspective. Because I tend to write down most things (I have journals that go back decades), I have a record of various events and circumstances. Our memories may fade, and very often do; our memories are often clouded, and sometimes our perceptions might be a little warped, but what you write down remains the same. When I am tempted to indulge in a pity-party at which I am the only guest, my journals become my reality check and remind me that I really have nothing to gripe about. I am confronted by evidence, in my own hand and in my own words, of God's goodness.

I liken life to a ladder, with each of us on different rungs. Wherever you might be at any given time, there will always be people above and behind you. There is one thing that life guarantees, that there will be challenges on the journey. No one is immune from the storms. They come when we least expect them, and they pass. We sometimes talk about our perception regarding the half-empty or half-full glass, but the other day something occurred to me. What if the glass were empty? If the glass were empty, then there would be nothing to work with. At least it has something in it! And as long as there is something in it, there is hope. We often compare ourselves to other people, or what we see of other people's lives. We think that we have been short-changed and convince ourselves that we would be happier, more fulfilled or more productive if only our circumstances were different. But as I have found, there is a lot to be thankful for, and the simple act of actually counting those blessings, big or small, will help you appreciate what you have. No matter what I go through, I have an awareness that there is someone who is worse off.

9.   Understand that you can have a dream and your dream can come true, regardless of your personal limitations.
My siblings and I were always encouraged to dream when we were children. I think I generally have a fertile imagination, but it was certainly stoked in the family in which I was planted. My parents taught us to dream. They constantly asked us what we wanted to be, what we wanted to do; it did not matter how old we were. Even if we changed our minds daily, they encouraged us to think about our futures, to think about the contribution that we would make to the world. We were not just another person, we were born to do something important.

I remember my three-year-old sister being asked what she would like to do when she was bigger. They listened very carefully when we would share those dreams, each one wilder than the ones that preceded. I remember that my sentences always began with, 'When I grow up, I want to be... When I grow up, I want to do...' I remember the indulgent looks on their faces as I spoke. But my dad always attached the realisation of the dream with working hard, and he always said, 'That is good, darling. You have to work very hard.' There was never any hint or suggestion that I may not achieve those dreams because I had a disability; in actual fact, the word did not exist in our home. My parents were our example, and because they both worked very hard and because we saw the results of their hard work, we connected the dots. Dreams + hard work = realisation and fulfilment.

I really believe that everybody should have a dream; everybody should be encouraged to dream. God encourages us to dream. He says: 'Write the vision And make *it* plain' (Habakkuk 2:2, NKJV). I believe that He wants us to dream; it is a means through which He communicates His plans for our lives. God-inspired dreams give you a picture of what is possible in spite of yourself! Most times they will be beyond your ability given your personal circumstances, and will require you to leave your comfort zone and reach for the unknown. Sometimes a dream may be so far removed from where you are presently that it is laughable; it may look impossible. But it is simply a picture of where you are going. It is like planning a holiday to a destination that you have never been to. You have a glossy travel brochure in your hand which shows several beautiful pictures of a sun-drenched paradise that almost causes you to salivate. On the basis of what you see, you take the necessary steps to get there: you buy a plane ticket, you take time off work, and you prepare to go. That is exactly how a dream is; you are shown a picture, and you begin the journey to get there.

I have found that the journey is exciting and breathtaking, and I have come to love the end result, when you finally hold in your hands what God saw from the very beginning.

10. Some of the biggest dreams have been birthed from uncommon tragedies and painful memories, so use your situation as a launching pad to greatness.

History is replete with examples of people who have done extraordinary things despite some very difficult circumstances. As I explained earlier, I recently discovered a flair for hymn-writing. It stemmed from my study of some of the most popular hymns which continue to bless successive generations hundreds of years after they were first written. I was intrigued by how powerful they were, and wondered at the depth of the writers' relationship with the Lord. What sort of relationship spawned such timeless words?

I was interested in the individuals behind the hymns, and soon noticed a common thread. A large number of them had been written during periods of great adversity. For instance, 'It is Well With My Soul', written by American lawyer Horatio Spafford (1828–88) was inspired by a series of traumatic experiences which culminated in the loss at sea of his four daughters. He had lost his only son a few years earlier. When he received news of the sinking of the passenger ship in which his family travelled, Spafford journeyed to reunite with his grieving wife, Anna, who had survived the tragic accident that had claimed their daughters' lives. As his ship passed the location where his daughters' ship had sunk, he penned the memorable and clearly divinely inspired words of that great hymn.

Today we sing this and other hymns, but each time I hear them I am challenged. How could someone be so optimistic in the midst of such tragedy? My mind struggles to understand the enormity of Spafford's loss. What makes a person so determined to keep going? Some might conclude that it points to a survival instinct, but I think it is more than that. I think that his response was that of someone who had a great awareness of something bigger than this world has to offer. And his eyes were on that bigger thing, and he drew strength from this awareness.

11. If you are comfortable with yourself, before long, the real you will shine through and others will be comfortable with you.

It has been my experience that people tend to take their cue from you. Rather than being uptight about your circumstance, it helps to be open about it. People are curious, and that curiosity can often lead them to say inappropriate things. Also, people generally don't know what to say or do and are concerned that they might say the wrong thing or cause offence.

I like the curiosity of children. They will ask awkward but honest questions, and I think that it is best to respond with openness. I have a gaggle of nieces and nephews of various ages. I noticed that they become aware round about the ages of six and seven. This is when they usually ask their parents, 'What happened to Aunty Chizor's arm?'

A few months ago, my seven-year-old niece was brought to me by her mother, who was clearly a little uncomfortable. My sister-in-law said, 'Mama wants to know what happened to your arm and I didn't know what to tell her.'

I took the little girl into the next room and asked her what she wanted to know.

'What happened to your arm, Aunty?' she asked.

I gave her the abridged version and allowed her to run her fingers over the scars on my arm. She looked a little sad for a moment, said, 'Sorry, Aunty', and gave me a hug. I told her that there was nothing to be sad about, that sometimes things happen but they should not stop you from being the best that you can be. I realised that this moment was a learning opportunity, and I hope my openness helped her to appreciate, as far as a seven-year-old can, the importance of being gentle with and accepting of people who might be different from her.

12. Go out of your way to make people feel comfortable. Help people understand your situation.

I was speaking to a young mother who is raising a child with a learning disability. On the whole, the parents were able to manage quite well, but sometimes the child was difficult to control, especially as he approached teenage years and got bigger and stronger.

One day the family was at their church, and were making their way out, along with other churchgoers after the service. Something had upset their child, who reacted by lashing out at his mother. Although she was not in any danger, and the situation resolved as quickly as it had flared up, no one had come to her aid; no one had intervened. There were several people around, but they appeared to have given them a wide berth. I noted the pain in the lady's words as she spoke about the incident; it was clear that she was very unhappy. I tried to place myself in the position of one of the people before whom this scene had played out. I was not sure that I would have acted any differently if I had found myself in a similar situation.

'What would you have wanted people to do? How would you have wanted them to respond?' I asked gently.

It turned out that she did not know; she simply wanted some acknowledgement of her struggles, to know that people were sensitive to her pain. Someone coming up to her to say, 'Are you all right?' would have been enough. No one wants to feel that they are invisible.

I understood what she was saying, but pointed out very carefully that people tend not to intervene because they do not know what to do, not because they do not want to help. People

181

do not want to make the situation worse, and because we are unsure what to do, the response is usually to avoid getting involved. I think that a two-way approach might be helpful. For the observer who sees something like this happening, a simple 'Are you OK? Do you need some help?' might be all that is needed. For the person on the other side, I think that it is important to send the message that offers of help would be greatly appreciated. These messages cannot be passed across without a conversation, and it would be the right time for some sort of dialogue to take place.

13. If the opportunity arises, be a voice for others.

It was my first year in a new position. I was still finding my feet and learning the ropes. I had heard about the wonderful team-bonding events that took place, and was looking forward to our summer bonding day. There was a team nominated specifically to plan an exciting and memorable event, and I waited like everyone to be surprised by what they had lined up for the staff. A week before the activity, an email was sent out with the relevant details. As I read the description of what was planned, I knew that it was an activity that I could not engage in fully or safely. I did not want to spoil the fun for others, and I thought about shrugging it off and just not turning up. But I knew that it would lead to numerous questions, and I also knew that it was my opportunity to educate my colleagues and to ensure that our future planning in whatever we did as an organisation and a community was guided by an awareness of and motivation towards inclusion.

When I pointed it out to the planning team, they were mortified. They meant no offence; it was just that it had not occurred to anyone. Someone actually said that they just did not view me as having a disability. Upon reflection, I thought that this was probably something positive; there were other aspects to me such that people could see past my disability. The learning for us all from that experience was that we had to work intentionally to ensure a more inclusive working environment, and that everything we did should not inadvertently discriminate against anyone.

Sometimes you might find yourself in a position of some influence where you can bring about change, whether big or small, for the benefit of other people.

It so happened that I had a voice. You are not given a voice to clamp your mouth shut and sit in silence. With a voice comes the responsibility of using it for the benefit of others who may not have a voice, or may not have one that has a reach where change can be effected. The Bible puts it this way: 'For everyone to whom much is given, from him much will be required; and to whom much has been committed, of him they will ask the more' (Luke 12:48, NKJV).

14. You have nothing to prove.
Over the last few months, I have bumped into a few people that I knew growing up and have been amazed at what they remembered about me. Each one made reference to the fact that I used to sprint then. I loved running, and I was always on athletic teams through my schooldays. Running was extremely liberating. There was just a sense of freedom that I experienced as I sliced through the wind. Whenever I ran I felt that I was competing on an equal footing, and in fact I was driven to show that I could challenge my able-bodied contemporaries. I tried desperately to be better than the opposition, and if ever there was no opposition, then I became my opposition, and I would try to better myself each time that I ran. The result was that I was extremely hard on myself, and I carried this into adulthood.

That sense of competition has never left me; it is both a benefit and a huge burden. Competition is only healthy when it spurs you on to give your best, and to strive to make advancements in whatever might be the relevant field for you. It becomes unhealthy when it drives you, and when it results from an irrational need to prove to yourself and to the world that you can contribute just as much or more than someone without your particular challenge. Most times in this latter case the competition is linked to one's sense of worth. As my relationship with the Lord has deepened, my sense of worth has increased in tandem, and my desire to prove myself has faded entirely. While I still drive myself, it is for the right reasons. I want to be the best that I can be, nothing more and nothing less!

15. Begin to see your disability as a 'mind-expanding' opportunity; an opportunity to expand your thinking – for example, through creativity.

Within the confines of disability lies great potential for creativity. Disabled people are often creative people, because they are compelled by their situations to think up creative ways of solving problems. They may be more inventive because of heightened imaginations; for instance, a blind man's other senses (hearing, smell, touch) are sharper in order to compensate for his lack of sight.

C. S. Lewis[5] spoke about vocations hidden within disability, which if they are discovered, could result in great personal gain thereby turning what was necessity into profit.

Because I enjoy painting, I am intrigued by the work of mouth and foot painting artists. I was quite fascinated to discover that there is a worldwide partnership of disabled artists who have taught themselves to paint with either mouth-held or foot-held brushes. I was interested in their individual stories and came across Mariam Paré, an American quadriplegic mouth artist who was disabled when she was caught in crossfire between rival Chicago-based gangs. She had attended art school as an able-bodied person, and continued painting despite having reduced mobility in her arms; she taught herself to paint with a brush held between her teeth. Ms Paré spoke of finding painting to be therapeutic, and how her art has provided joy from suffering.

Looking at a disability as a potential source for creativity can have far-reaching consequences which one could never fully anticipate.

16. Whatever you do, steer clear of people and situations that constantly put you down.
I think that life has enough challenges and that an individual, disabled or not, goes through enough internal struggles without taking on the additional burden of unhealthy relationships or unhealthy environments. Some time ago, I heard a statement that upon reflection made a lot of sense. The person speaking at the time said: 'Go where you are celebrated.' In other words, do not subject yourself to situations or relationships which hack away at your confidence or sense of worth. As far as you are able, surround yourself with people who will build you up, correct you lovingly, and support your progress.

The other day I saw a programme advertised that highlighted people who were living with a challenge or disability and who were searching for romance. The title of the programme questioned whether they were too unattractive to find love. I watched the first run of the programme and felt saddened by what I saw and heard. I could hear raw pain in voices as the individuals with a range of physical challenges described their feelings of inadequacy, self-doubt and anxiety. I saw their angst as they agonised over whether to tell their dates about their conditions at the first meeting. After a while, I was practically screaming at the television screen, 'You're too uptight. Too intense. Lighten up. You'll make him run a mile in the opposite direction. It's not that big a deal! You are more than a disability or an ailment!' Of course, when the dates did not call a second time, then there was the whole self-fulfilling prophecy at play, and the individuals felt more distressed, more lonely and more inadequate. Long after the final credits had rolled, my thoughts were still consumed by the programme. Why would anyone with a fragile personality and who clearly struggled with issues of self-esteem place themselves in a position which highlighted the very things that caused those insecurities, leaving themselves exposed and open to potential rejection?

There is a person, a living, breathing person with feelings and great potential behind every physical condition. Whatever you do, don't inadvertently sabotage your own progress.

17. It is very likely that you will experience the best and the worst of human nature.

I have always struggled to comprehend the depravity of individuals who attack weak and vulnerable people. Whenever I hear a story of a disabled child or adult being abused, physically or emotionally, it causes my hackles to rise. I think I would really love an opportunity to sit in front of those bullying people and try to ascertain what motivates such callous behaviour.

During my research on Alison Lapper, I was shocked to read her account of some of the prejudices that she encountered. She spoke of an incident during her pregnancy when she went into a pharmacy to have a prescription filled. Two elderly women also present in the store spoke within earshot questioning why someone in her position, who in their opinion was obviously a burden on the taxpayer, would dare to bring a child into the world, thus increasing society's burden. They knew nothing about her, nothing about her pursuit of independence, or the fact that she earned a living as an artist and lecturer, but they saw nothing wrong in making uninformed judgements nonetheless.

Whilst such incidences are harrowing and harsh comments carry a stinging blow, it is important to appreciate that though there are unkind people walking around, there are also wonderful people with big hearts. Thankfully I have met so many more people in this latter group, and my encounter with the few in the former only served to strengthen my resolve and spur me on to push even harder at boundaries.

I conclude with these words which continue to impact my life greatly:

> In the presence of trouble, some people grow wings, others buy crutches.
> Harold W. Ruoff[6]

---

[1] Eryn Sun, 'Joni Eareckson Tada on Wilberforce Award "Better Off Dead Than Disabled" Mentality', 16th March 2012. Available at http://www.christianpost.com/news/joni-eareckson-tada-on-wilberforce-award-better-off-dead-than-disabled-mentality-71536/ (accessed 21st September 2015).

[2] Susan King, *Los Angeles Times*: 'Garr back on her feet, back on the big screen', 30th June 2008, http://articles.latimes.com/2008/jun/30/entertainment/et-garr30 (accessed 25th May 2015).

[3] Mark Twain, cited in Larry Chang (ed), *Wisdom for the Soul: Five Millennia of Prescriptions for Spiritual Healing* (Washington: Gnosophia Publishers), p. 478.

[4] Friedrich Nietzsche, German philosopher.

---

[5] Clive Staples Lewis, commonly known as C. S. Lewis (1898–1963) novelist, poet, broadcaster. Author of several works of fantasy literature, including *The Chronicles of Narnia.*

[6] In John L. Mason, *You're Born an Original, Don't Die a Copy!* (Tulsa, OK: Insight International, 1993) p.62.

Prayer

Jesus came into the world to save you and me from the consequences of our wrongdoing. He took the punishment that was to be ours by dying on the cross because He loves us. He rose from the dead and ascended into heaven but He left us His Spirit as our guide.

If you would like to get to know Jesus, then you can begin a relationship with Him by saying these simple words:

Lord Jesus, I believe that You are the Son of God and that You came to the world and died for my sins. I believe that You love me and I ask that You come into my life from this moment on. Thank you.
Amen.

Timeline

I was born in Nigeria in 1967. I was brought to England at age seven for medical treatment at St Mary's Hospital, Paddington and was here for a year, following which I returned to Nigeria. In this year in London, I had three quite extensive surgeries on my arm. My mum was with me for each surgery and for several days afterwards, but she had to return to Nigeria to work and to be with the rest of the family, so she left me with her cousin, Aunty Mercy. I lived with her for the year.

From age 11 my parents took me to Boston, Massachusetts for further medical treatment at Massachusetts General Hospital. There were several surgeries over a number of years, and I was away from home (Nigeria) for months at a time for each round of treatment, which included the surgery and the post-operation therapy. Where possible the surgeries would be fixed to coincide with holiday periods so that I did not miss much of school, but it required several weeks and sometimes months for the pre-op evaluations, the actual surgery, recovery period, and post-operation therapy. So on average in a year I would be away from home in Nigeria for between three to six months.

At age 15 my parents sent me and my brother Ikechi, who is 19 months older, to England to continue our education. Our older brother, Agu, had preceded us to the UK two years earlier, and my younger sisters would come a few years later. It was always my parents' desire to give us a good education and they believed that the English boarding school system provided this.

My brother and I attended a boarding school in West Cumbria. I was there for three years. The summer before I began at the school, I had more surgery in the USA and started the new term with a plaster cast; the doctors had cleared me to return to England so that I did not miss out on the start of the school year at a new school, but I had to return to the USA a few weeks later to have the cast and some metal pins removed. My mother came from Nigeria, got me from school and took me to Boston for this, and afterwards returned me to England.

After completing my A-Levels, I went to Warwick University and then Nottingham University (Bachelor of Laws and Master of Laws degrees respectively). I then went to art college (in 1991) for a year to fulfil a burning desire. The following year, in 1992, I returned to Nigeria to attend the Nigerian Law School and sit the Bar examinations. After I qualified as a barrister and solicitor in Nigeria I returned to the UK and subsequently qualified as a solicitor in England and Wales several years later.

Bajo and I got married in January 1997. We travelled to Nigeria for our wedding and returned afterwards to set up home in Brighton, East Sussex. Risachi was born a year later (January 1998) and Rinnah was born in August 2000, both in Brighton. We had a miscarriage in November 2008 and a stillbirth (Jedidiah) in September of the following year.

I was ordained as a pastor of the Redeemed Christian Church of God in 2006.

I resigned from my position overseeing a criminal litigation department in 2010 and in September 2012 I was offered the position of general manager at my church, Jesus House London and began working there in February of the following year.

About the author

When Chizor Akisanya is asked to speak about herself, she struggles to find the words. Then she smiles as though a thought has just occurred to her, and says, 'I'm special.' She is grateful for a strong and supportive family environment which was the backdrop to her early years. During her adolescence, when acceptance was a crucial issue for a teenager's development, she had an experience in which the Lord told her that she was special. Wrapped up in those few words were the strength and encouragement that she needed to strive for a life of maximised potential.

Today, opportunities are opening up for her to reach people, particularly young women, with the Christian message of love. She is well on the way to becoming an advocate for people living with disabilities, and is keen to raise awareness of disability issues within the Church community. As a solicitor, she practised law for several years, and recently took on a senior management position at Jesus House London, which is a parish of the Redeemed Christian Church of God. She is an ordained pastor, artist, author, with a particular interest in hymn-writing, a speaker and mentor to women of varying ages.

She is married to Bajo, and they have two teenage daughters, Risachi and Rinnah. *Complete in Him* is her first published work.